FIRST 50 FOLK SONGS
YOU SHOULD PLAY ON THE GUITAR

ISBN 978-1-4950-9564-1

HAL•LEONARD®
7777 W. BLUEMOUND RD. P.O. BOX 13819 MILWAUKEE, WI 53213

In Australia Contact:
Hal Leonard Australia Pty. Ltd.
4 Lentara Court
Cheltenham, Victoria, 3192 Australia
Email: ausadmin@halleonard.com.au

Visit Hal Leonard Online at
www.halleonard.com

CONTENTS

4 .... Amazing Grace	36 .... Michael Row the Boat Ashore
5 .... Arkansas Traveler	38 .... Midnight Special
6 .... Barbara Allen	40 .... My Old Kentucky Home
7 .... Beautiful Brown Eyes	37 .... Nobody Knows the Trouble I've Seen
8 .... Buffalo Gals (Won't You Come Out Tonight?)	42 .... Oh! Susanna
9 .... Bury Me Not on the Lone Prairie	44 .... Old Folks at Home (Swanee River)
10 .... Cindy	43 .... The Red River Valley
11 .... Corrina	46 .... Rock Island Line
12 .... The Crawdad Song	48 .... Scarborough Fair
14 .... (I Wish I Was In) Dixie	50 .... She Wore a Yellow Ribbon
16 .... Down by the Riverside	49 .... She'll Be Comin' 'Round the Mountain
13 .... Down in the Valley	52 .... Sometimes I Feel Like a Motherless Child
18 .... Freight Train	54 .... There Is a Tavern in the Town
19 .... Good Night Ladies	53 .... This Little Light of Mine
20 .... Hesitation Blues	56 .... This Train
22 .... Home on the Range	58 .... Turkey in the Straw
24 .... I've Been Working on the Railroad	57 .... The Wabash Cannon Ball
21 .... In the Good Old Summertime	60 .... Water Is Wide
26 .... John Brown's Body	61 .... When Johnny Comes Marching Home
28 .... John Henry	62 .... When the Saints Go Marching In
30 .... Kumbaya	63 .... Wildwood Flower
31 .... Little Brown Jug	64 .... Will the Circle Be Unbroken
32 .... Make Me a Pallet on the Floor	65 .... Worried Man Blues
33 .... Man of Constant Sorrow	68 .... Yankee Doodle
34 .... Matty Groves	66 .... The Yellow Rose of Texas

Amazing Grace

Words by John Newton
From a Collection of Sacred Ballads
Traditional American Melody
From Carrell and Clayton's Virginia Harmony
Arranged by Edwin O. Excell

Additional Lyrics

2. 'Twas grace that taught my heart to fear,
And grace my fears relieved.
How precious did that grace appear
The hour I first believed.

3. Through many dangers, toils and snares,
I have already come.
'Tis grace hath brought me safe thus far,
And grace will lead me home.

4. The Lord has promised good to me,
His Word my hope secures.
He will my shield and portion be,
As long as life endures.

5. And when this flesh and heart shall fail,
And mortal life shall cease,
I shall possess, within the veil
A life of joy and peace.

6. When we've been there ten thousand years,
Bright shining as the sun,
We've no less days to sing God's praise
Than when we'd first begun.

Arkansas Traveler

Southern American Folksong

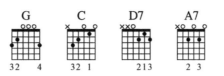

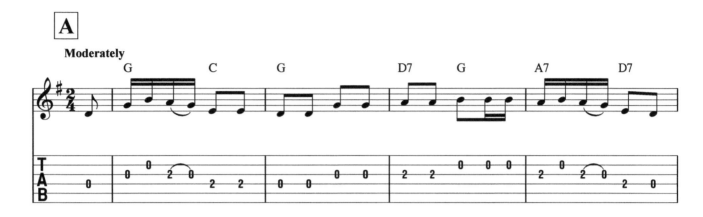

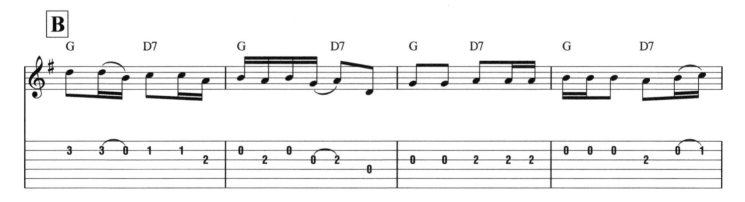

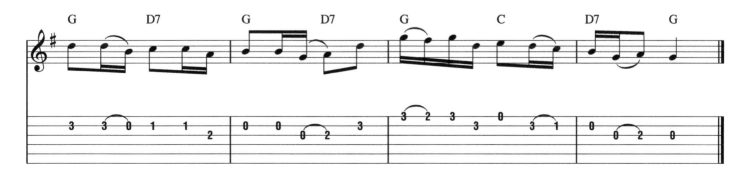

Barbara Allen

Traditional English

Additional Lyrics

2. 'Twas in the merry month of May,
When green buds they were swellin'.
Sweet William on his deathbed lay
For love of Barb'ra Allen.

3. He sent a servant to the town,
The place where she was dwellin'.
"My master's sick and bids you come
If you be Barb'ra Allen."

4. And as she crossed the wooded fields,
She heard his death bell knellin'.
And ev'ry stroke, it spoke her name,
"Hardhearted Barb'ra Allen."

5. "Oh Mother, Mother, make my bed,
And make it long and narrow.
Sweet William died for love of me;
I'll die for him of sorrow."

6. "Farewell," she said, "ye maidens all,
And shun the fault I fell in:
Henceforth take warning by the fall
Of cruel Barb'ra Allen."

Beautiful Brown Eyes

Traditional

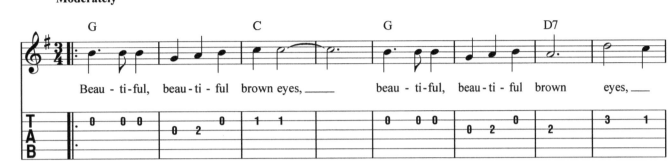

Chorus
Moderately

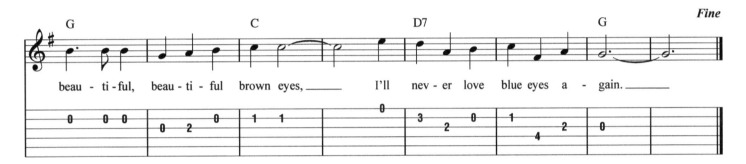

Beau - ti - ful, beau - ti - ful brown eyes, _____ beau - ti - ful, beau - ti - ful brown eyes, _____

Fine

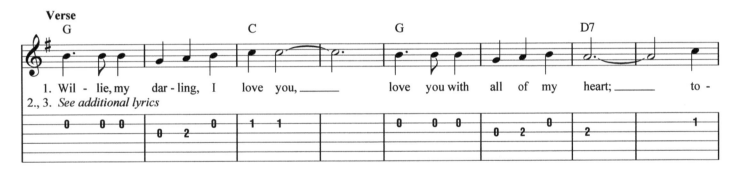

beau - ti - ful, beau - ti - ful brown eyes, _____ I'll nev - er love blue eyes a - gain. _____

Verse

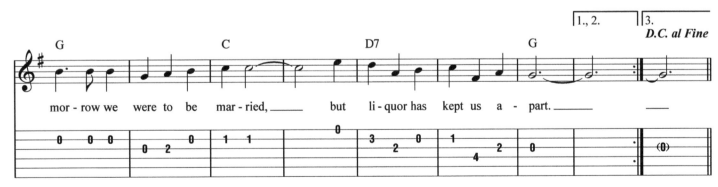

1. Wil - lie, my dar - ling, I love you, _____ love you with all of my heart; _____ to -
2., 3. *See additional lyrics*

|1., 2. |3.
D.C. al Fine

mor - row we were to be mar - ried, _____ but li - quor has kept us a - part. _____ _____

Additional Lyrics

2. I staggered into the barroom.
   I fell down on the floor.
   And the very last words I uttered,
   "I'll never get drunk anymore."

3. Seven long years I've been married,
   I wish I was single again,
   A woman don't know half her troubles
   Until she has married a man.

Buffalo Gals
(Won't You Come Out Tonight?)

Words and Music by Cool White (John Hodges)

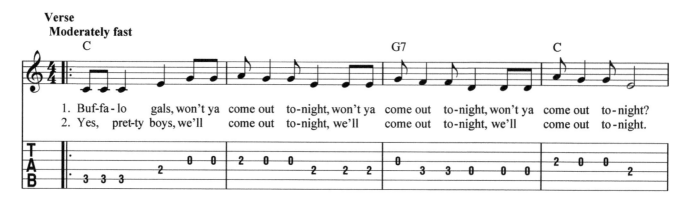

Verse
Moderately fast

1. Buf-fa-lo gals, won't ya come out to-night, won't ya come out to-night, won't ya come out to-night?
2. Yes, pret-ty boys, we'll come out to-night, we'll come out to-night, we'll come out to-night.

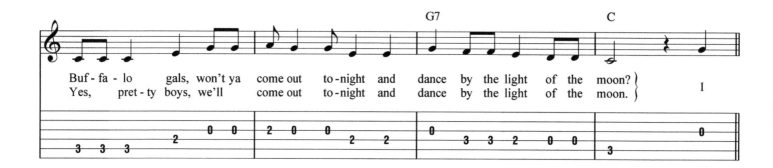

Buf-fa-lo gals, won't ya come out to-night and dance by the light of the moon?
Yes, pret-ty boys, we'll come out to-night and dance by the light of the moon.

Chorus

danced with a gal with a hole in her stock-ing and her heel kept a rock-in' and her toe kept a knock-in'. I

danced with a gal with a hole in her stock-ing, and we danced by the light of the moon. moon.

Bury Me Not on the Lone Prairie

Words based on the poem "The Ocean Burial" by Rev. Edwin H. Chapin
Music by Ossian N. Dodge

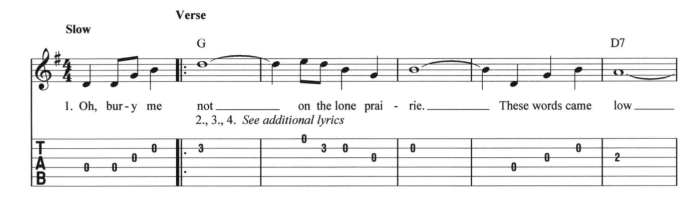

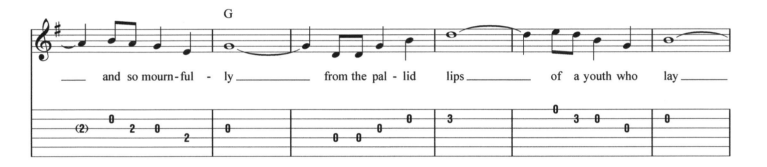

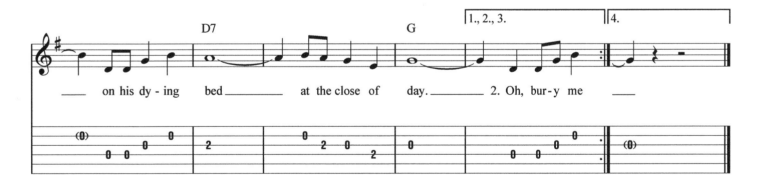

Additional Lyrics

2. Oh, bury me not on the lone prairie
Where the coyotes howl and the wind blows free;
In a narrow grave just six by three,
Oh, bury me not on the lone prairie.

3. "Oh, bury me not," and his voice failed there.
But we took no heed to his dying prayer;
In a narrow grave just six by three,
We buried him there on the lone prairie.

4. Yes, we buried him there on the lone prairie
Where the owl all night hoots mournfully;
And the blizzard beats and the wind blows free,
O'er his lonely grave on the lone prairie.

Cindy

Southern Appalachian Folksong

Additional Lyrics

2. I wish I was an apple,
A hangin' from a tree.
And ev'ry time that Cindy passed,
She'd take a bite of me.

3. I wish I was a rich guy,
With cash in several banks.
I sure would buy nice things for her,
To hear her whisper, "Thanks."

4. I wish that I were single,
I wish that I were free.
So I could change this dream of mine
Into reality.

Corrina

Traditional

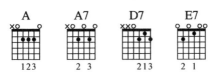

Verse

Moderately

1. Cor - ri - na, Cor - ri - na, where you been so long?
   ri - na, where'd you stay last night?
   ri - na, way a - cross the sea,
   4. - 9. *See additional lyrics*

Cor-ri - na, Cor - ri - na, where you been so long? Ain't had no
Cor-ri - na, Cor - ri - na, where'd you stay last night? Come in this
I met Cor - ri - na, way a - cross the sea. She would-n't write no

lov - ing, since you been gone. 2. Cor - ri - na, Cor -
morn - ing, sun was shin - ing bright. 3. I met Cor -
let - ter, she did-n't care for me. 4. Cor - ri - na, Cor -

Additional Lyrics

4. Corrina, Corrina, what you gonna do?
   Corrina, Corrina, what you gonna do?
   Just a little bit of loving, let your heart be true.

5. I love Corrina, tell the world I do,
   I love Corrina, tell the world I do,
   Just a little bit of loving, let your heart be true.

6. Corrina, Corrina, dear pal of mine,
   Corrina, Corrina, dear pal of mine,
   Now she left walking, tears rolling and crying.

7. Corrina, Corrina, what's the matter now?
   Corrina, Corrina, what's the matter now?
   You wouldn't write me no letters, you don't love me no how.

8. Good-bye, Corrina, it's fare you well.
   Good-bye, Corrina, it's fare you well.
   When I get back here, can't anyone tell.

9. Got a bird that whistles, I got a bird that sings,
   Got a bird that whistles, I got a bird that sings,
   But I ain't got Corrina, life don't mean a thing.

The Crawdad Song

Traditional

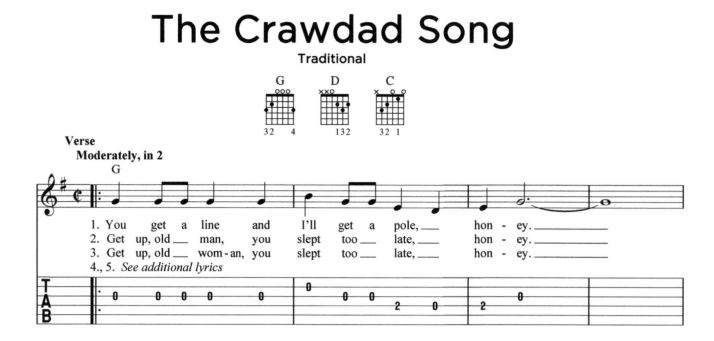

Verse
Moderately, in 2

1. You get a line and I'll get a pole, ____ hon - ey. ____
2. Get up, old ___ man, you slept too ___ late, ____ hon - ey. ____
3. Get up, old ___ wom-an, you slept too ___ late, ____ hon - ey. ____
4., 5. *See additional lyrics*

You get a line and I'll get a pole, ____ babe. ____
Get up, old ___ man, you slept too ___ late, ____ babe. ____
Get up, old ___ wom-an, you slept too ___ late, ____ babe. ____

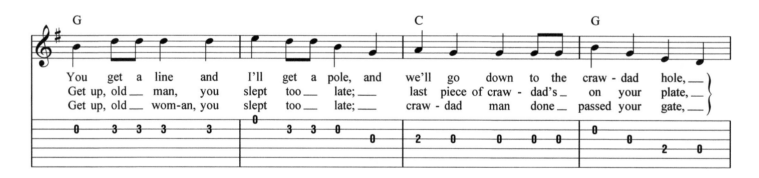

You get a line and I'll get a pole, and we'll go down to the craw - dad hole, ____
Get up, old ___ man, you slept too ___ late; ____ last piece of craw - dad's ___ on your plate, ____
Get up, old ___ wom-an, you slept too ___ late; ____ craw - dad man done ___ passed your gate, ____

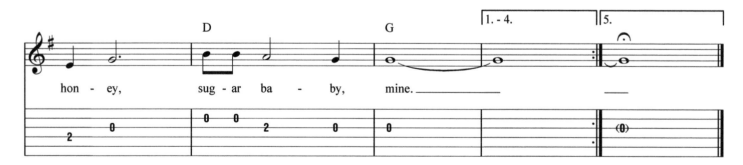

hon - ey, sug - ar ba - by, mine. ____

Additional Lyrics

4. Along come a man with a sack on his back, honey.
   Along come a man with a sack on his back, babe,
   Along come a man with a sack on his back,
   Packin' all the crawdads he can pack, honey, sugar baby, mine.

5. What you gonna do when the lake goes dry, honey?
   What you gonna do when the lake goes dry, babe?
   What you gonna do when the lake goes dry?
   Sit on the bank and watch the crawdads die, honey, sugar baby, mine.

Down in the Valley

Traditional American Folksong

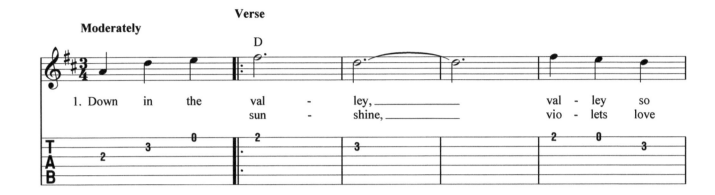

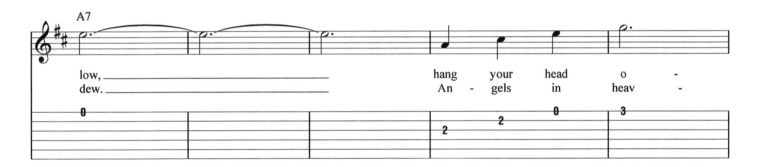

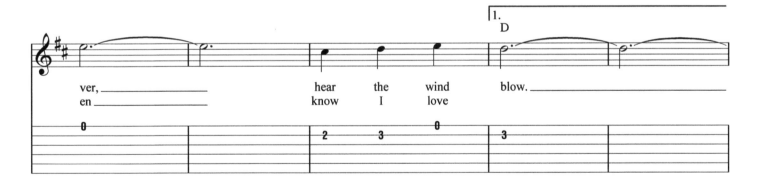

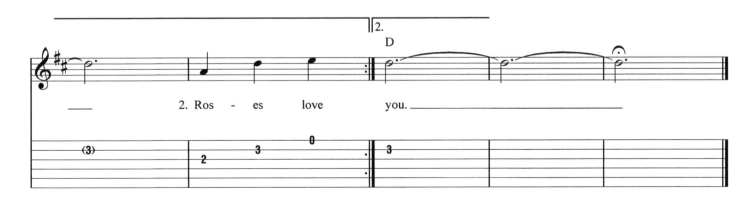

(I Wish I Was In) Dixie

Words and Music by Daniel Decatur Emmett

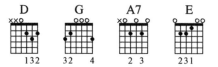

Fast

Verse

1. I ___ wish I was ___ in the land of cot - ton.
2. *See additional lyrics*

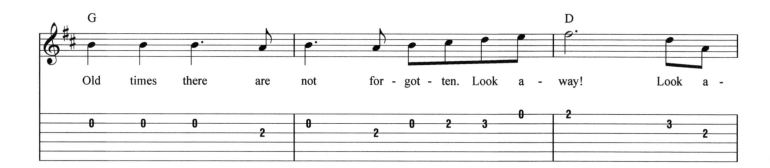

Old times there are not for - got - ten. Look a - way! Look a -

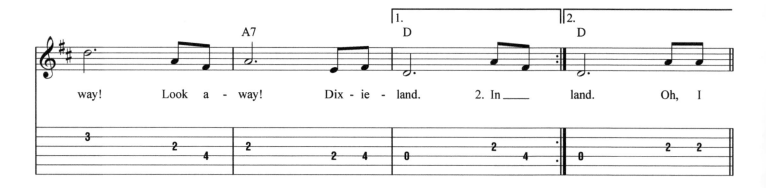

way! Look a - way! Dix - ie - land. 2. In ___ land. Oh, I

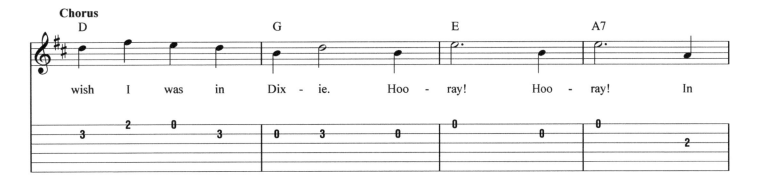

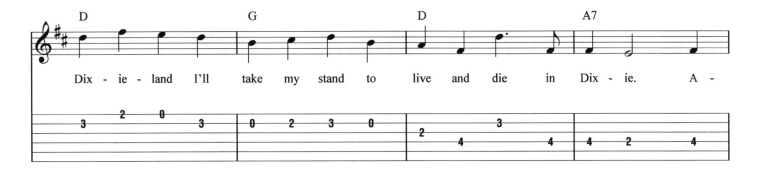

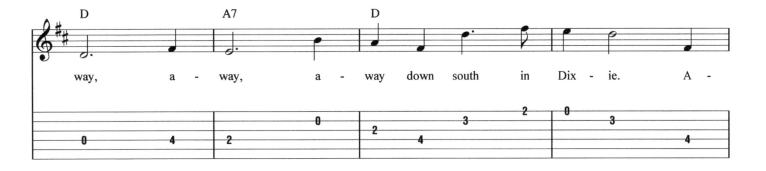

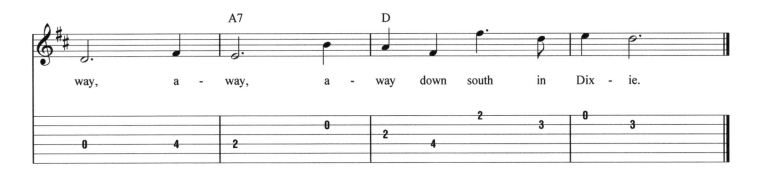

Additional Lyrics

2. In Dixieland where I was born in,
   Early on one frosty mornin',
   Look away! Look away!
   Look away! Dixieland.

Down by the Riverside

African American Spiritual

Verse
Moderately, in 2

1. Gon - na lay down my sword and shield _ down by the
2., 3., 4. *See additional lyrics*

riv - er - side, _ down by the riv - er - side, _ down by the

riv - er - side. _ Gon - na lay down my sword and shield _ down by the

riv - er - side, _ and stud - y _____ war no more. _____ I ain't gon - na

Additional Lyrics

2. I'm gonna join hands with everyone
Down by the riverside, down by the riverside,
Down by the riverside.
I'm gonna join hands with everyone
Down by the riverside,
And study war no more.

3. I'm gonna put on my long white robe
Down by the riverside, down by the riverside,
Down by the riverside.
I'm gonna put on my long white robe
Down by the riverside,
And study war no more.

4. I'm gonna walk with the Prince of Peace
Down by the riverside, down by the riverside,
Down by the riverside.
I'm gonna walk with the Prince of Peace
Down by the riverside,
And study war no more.

Freight Train

Words and Music by Elizabeth Cotten

Additional Lyrics

3. When I die, Lord, bury me deep,
   Way down on old Chestnut Street.
   So I can hear old Number Nine
   As she comes rolling by.

Good Night Ladies

Words by E.P. Christy
Traditional Music

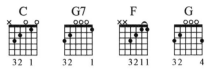

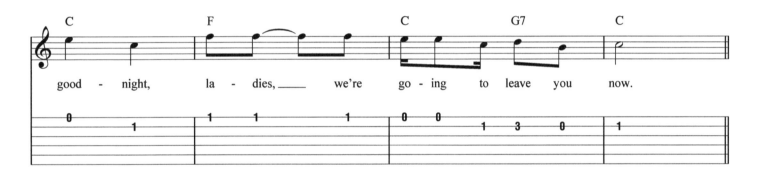

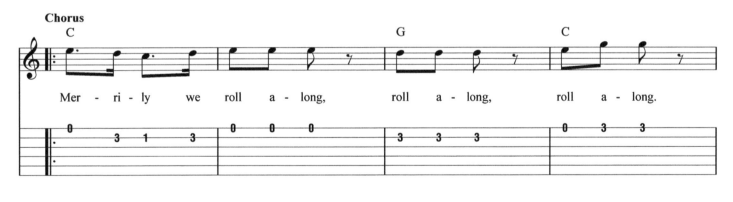

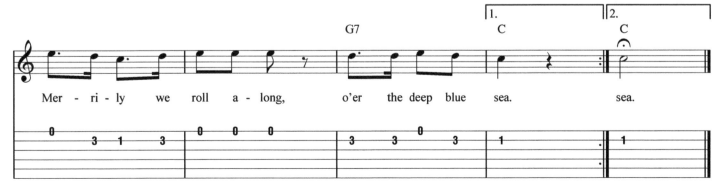

Hesitation Blues

Words and Music by Billy Smythe and J. Scott Middleton

Additional Lyrics

2. Well, the eagle on the dollar say, "In God we trust,"
   Woman wants a man, she wants to see a dollar first...

3. Ashes to ashes, dust to dust,
   I've got a black-haired mama that the rains can't rust...

4. Well, you hesitate by one, and you hesitate by two,
   Angels up in heaven singing hesitatin' blues...

In the Good Old Summertime

Words by Ren Shields
Music by George Evans

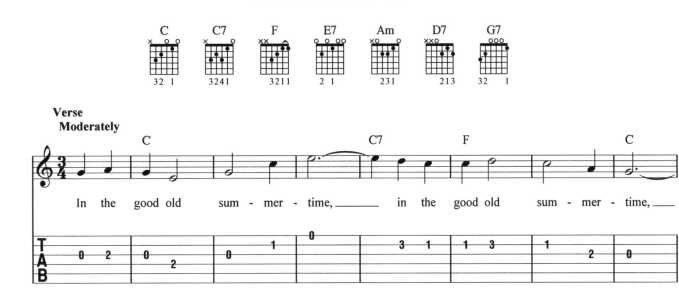

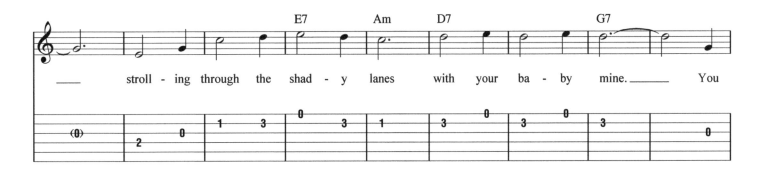

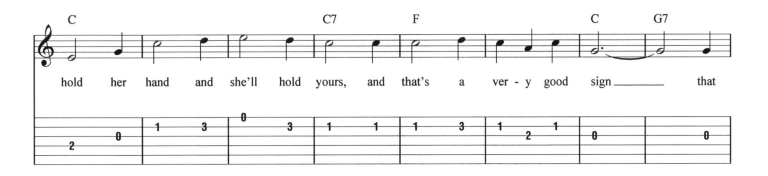

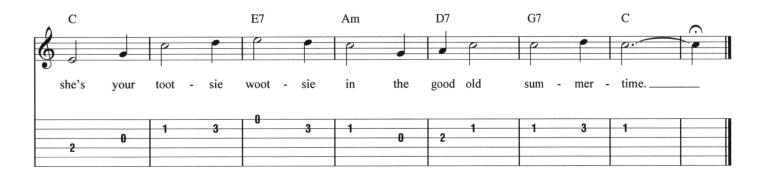

Home on the Range

Lyrics by Dr. Brewster Higley
Music by Dan Kelly

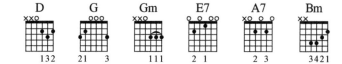

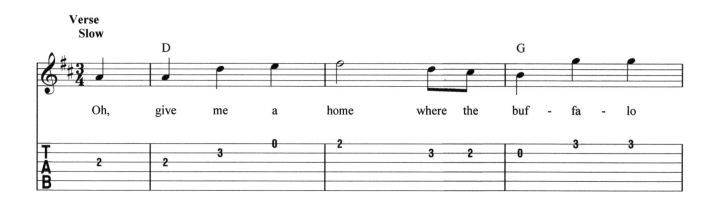

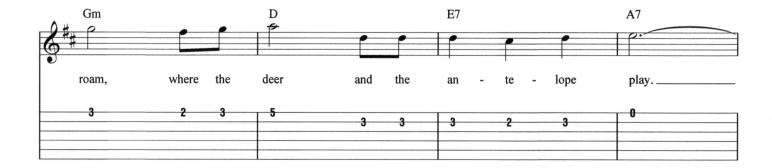

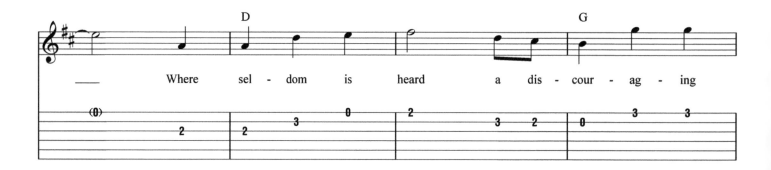

word, and the skies are not cloud - y all day._____

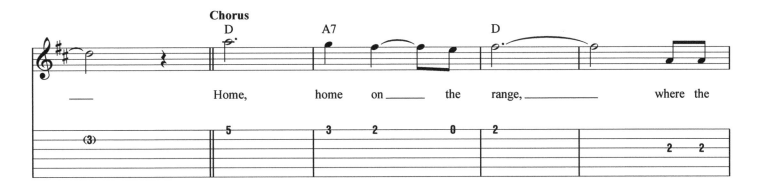

Chorus

_____ Home, home on _____ the range, _____ where the

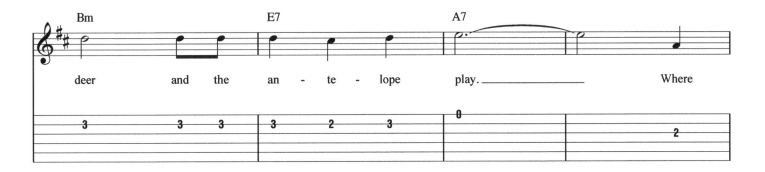

deer and the an - te - lope play._____ Where

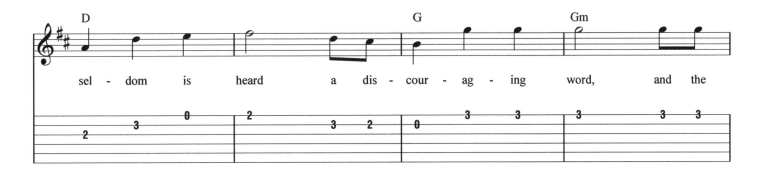

sel - dom is heard a dis - cour - ag - ing word, and the

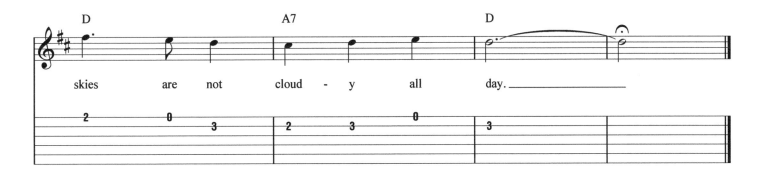

skies are not cloud - y all day._____

I've Been Working on the Railroad

American Folksong

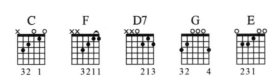

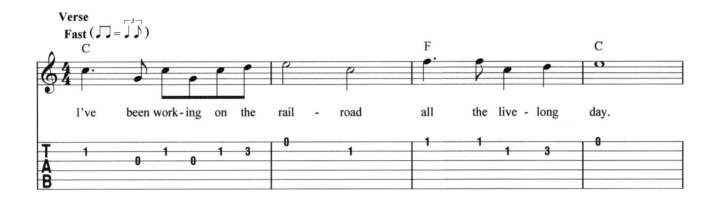

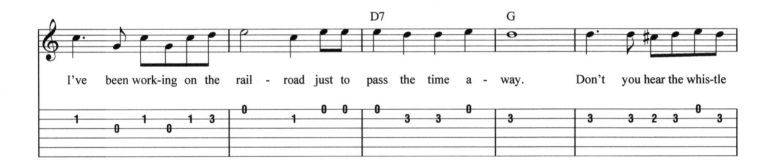

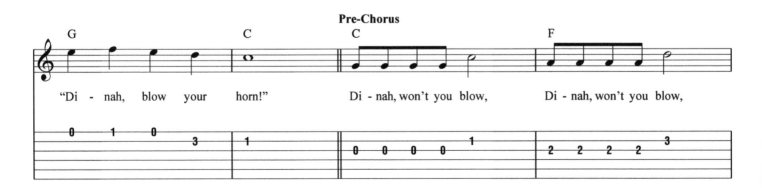

John Brown's Body

Traditional

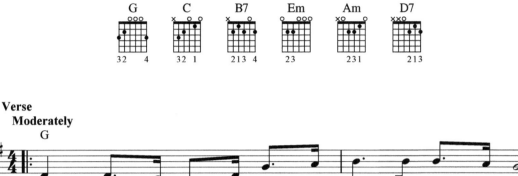

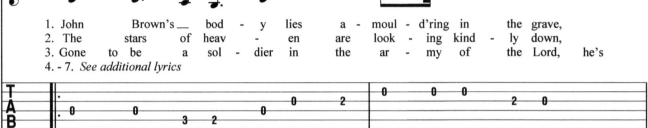

Verse
Moderately

1. John Brown's bod - y lies a - moul - d'ring in the grave,
2. The stars of heav - en are look - ing kind - ly down,
3. Gone to be a sol - dier in the ar - my of the Lord, he's
4. - 7. *See additional lyrics*

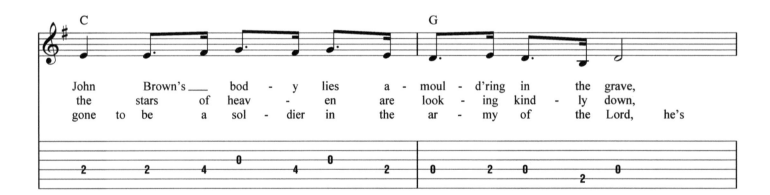

John Brown's bod - y lies a - moul - d'ring in the grave,
the stars of heav - en are look - ing kind - ly down,
gone to be a sol - dier in the ar - my of the Lord, he's

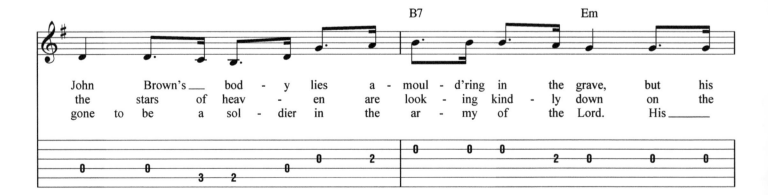

John Brown's bod - y lies a - moul - d'ring in the grave, but his
the stars of heav - en are look - ing kind - ly down on the
gone to be a sol - dier in the ar - my of the Lord. His

Additional Lyrics

4. John Brown died that the slave might be free,
   John Brown died that the slave might be free,
   John Brown died that the slave might be free,
   But his soul goes marching on.

5. John Brown's knapsack is strapped to his back,
   John Brown's knapsack is strapped to his back,
   John Brown's knapsack is strapped to his back.
   His soul is marching on.

6. His pet lambs will meet on the way,
   His pet lambs will meet on the way,
   His pet lambs will meet on the way,
   And they'll go marching on.

7. They will hang Jeff Davis on a sour apple tree,
   They will hang Jeff Davis on a sour apple tree,
   They will hang Jeff Davis on a sour apple tree
   As they go marching on.

John Henry

West Virginia Folksong

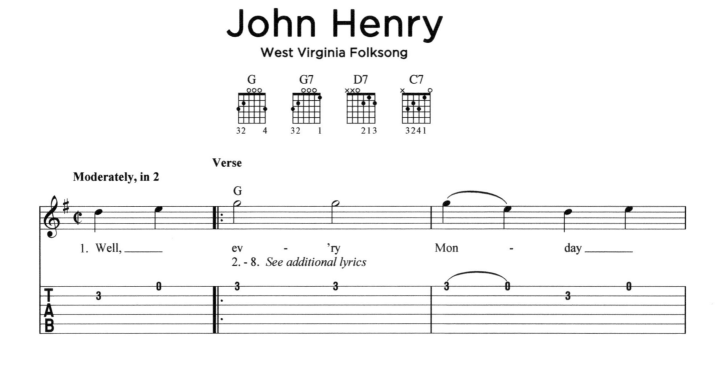

Verse

Moderately, in 2

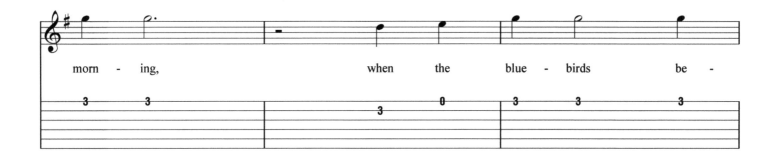

1. Well, _____ ev - 'ry Mon - day _____
2. - 8. *See additional lyrics*

morn - ing, when the blue - birds be -

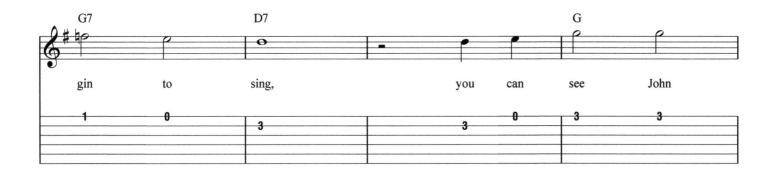

gin to sing, you can see John

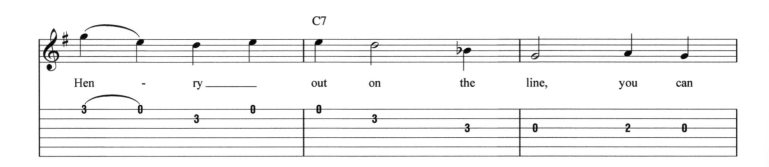

Hen - ry _____ out on the line, you can

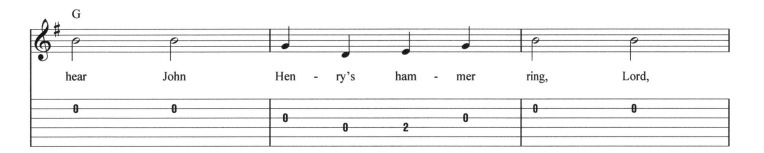

hear   John   Hen - ry's   ham - mer   ring,   Lord,

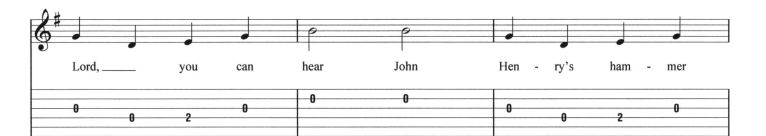

Lord, _____   you   can   hear   John   Hen - ry's   ham - mer

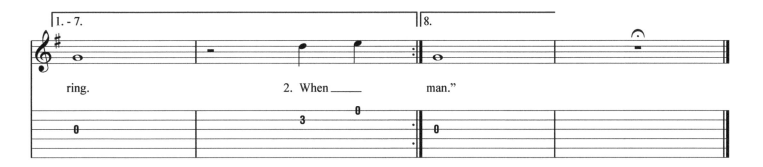

ring.   2. When _____   man."

Additional Lyrics

2. When John Henry was a little baby
   A sitting on his papa's knee,
   He picked up a hammer and a little piece of steel,
   Said, "Hammer's gonna be the death of me, Lord, Lord,
   Hammer's gonna be the death of me."

3. Well, the Captain said to John Henry,
   "Gonna bring me a steam drill 'round,
   Gonna bring me a steam drill out on the job,
   Gonna whip that steel on down, Lord, Lord,
   Gonna whip that steel on down."

4. John Henry said to his captain,
   "A man ain't nothin' but a man,
   And before I let that steam drill beat me down,
   I'll die with my hammer in my hand, Lord, Lord,
   I'll die with my hammer in my hand."

5. John Henry said to his shaker,
   "Shaker, why don't you pray?
   'Cause if I miss this little piece of steel,
   Tomorrow be your buryin' day, Lord, Lord,
   Tomorrow be your buryin' day."

6. John Henry was drivin' on the mountain
   And his hammer was flashing fire.
   But he hammered so hard that he broke his poor heart,
   "Gimme a cool drink of water 'fore I die, Lord, Lord,
   Gimme a cool drink of water 'fore I die."

7. John Henry, he drove fifteen feet,
   The steam drill made only nine,
   And the last words I heard the poor boy say,
   And he laid down his hammer and he died, Lord, Lord,
   And he laid down his hammer and he died.

8. They took John Henry to the graveyard
   And buried him in the sand
   And every locomotive comes a roaring by says,
   "There lies a steel driving man, Lord, Lord,
   There lies a steel driving man."

Kumbaya

Congo Folksong

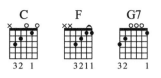

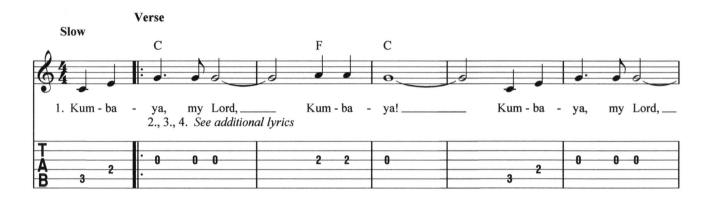

Verse

Slow

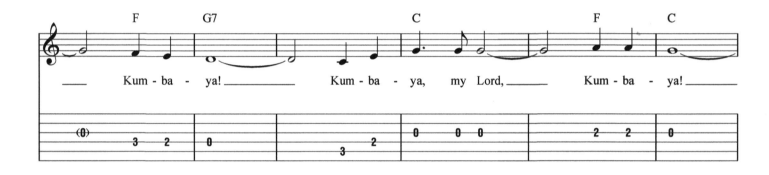

1. Kum - ba - ya, my Lord, _____ Kum - ba - ya! _____ Kum - ba - ya, my Lord, _____
2., 3., 4. *See additional lyrics*

_____ Kum - ba - ya! _____ Kum - ba - ya, my Lord, _____ Kum - ba - ya! _____

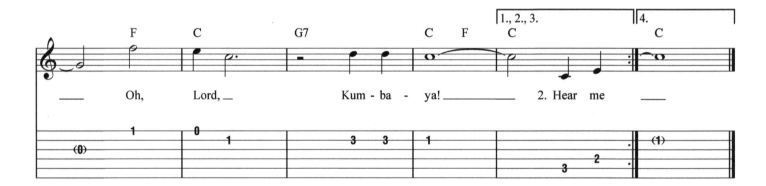

_____ Oh, Lord, _____ Kum - ba - ya! _____ 2. Hear me

Additional Lyrics

2. Hear me crying, Lord, Kumbaya!
   Hear me crying, Lord, Kumbaya!
   Hear me crying, Lord, Kumbaya!
   Oh, Lord, Kumbaya!

3. Hear me praying, Lord, Kumbaya!
   Hear me praying, Lord, Kumbaya!
   Hear me praying, Lord, Kumbaya!
   Oh, Lord! Kumbaya!

4. Oh, I need you, Lord, Kumbaya!
   Oh, I need you, Lord, Kumbaya!
   Oh, I need you, Lord, Kumbaya!
   Oh, Lord, Kumbaya!

Little Brown Jug

Words and Music by Joseph E. Winner

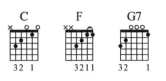

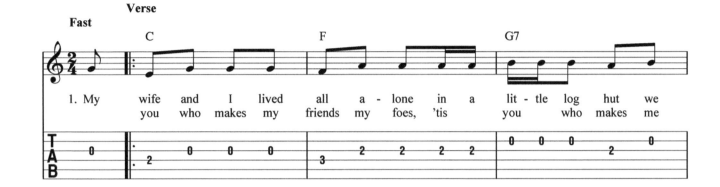

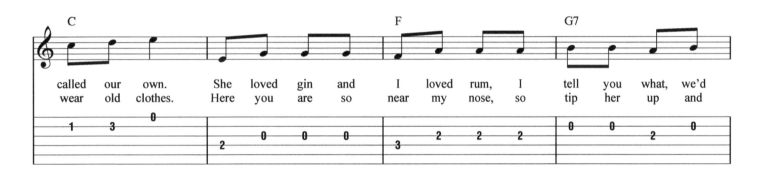

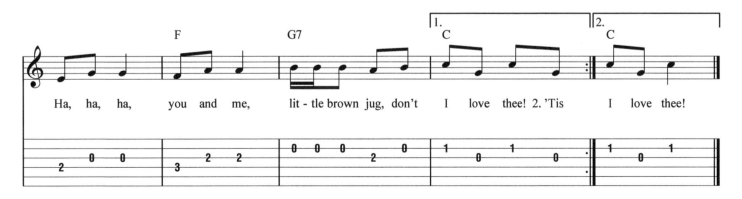

Make Me a Pallet on the Floor

Traditional

Additional Lyrics

4. Don't you let my good girl catch you here.
Don't you let my good girl catch you here.
She might shoot you, cut and stab you, too.
Ain't no telling just what she might do.

Man of Constant Sorrow

Traditional

Additional Lyrics

2. For six long years I've been in trouble,
   No pleasure here on earth I found.
   For in this world I'm bound to ramble,
   I have no friends to help me now.

3. It's fare you well, my own true lover,
   I never expect to see you again;
   For I'm bound to ride that northern railroad,
   Perhaps I'll die upon this train.

4. You may bury me in some deep valley,
   For many years where I may lay.
   Then you may learn to love another,
   While I am sleeping in my grave.

5. Maybe your friends think I'm just a stranger,
   My face, you never will see no more.
   But there is one promise that is given,
   I'll meet you on God's golden shore.

Matty Groves

English Folksong

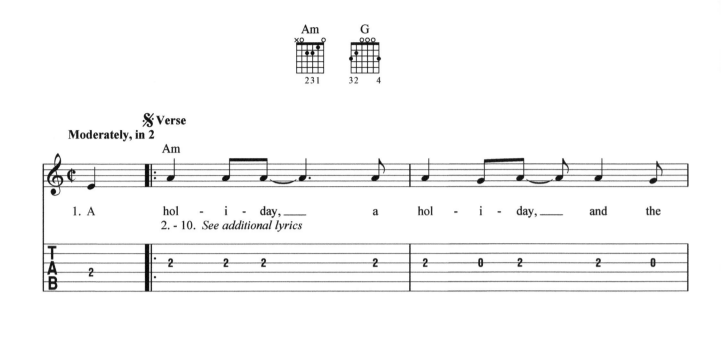

Moderately, in 2

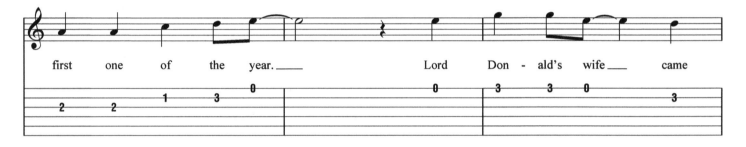

1. A hol - i - day, _____ a hol - i - day, _____ and the
2. - 10. *See additional lyrics*

first one of the year. _____ Lord Don - ald's wife _____ came

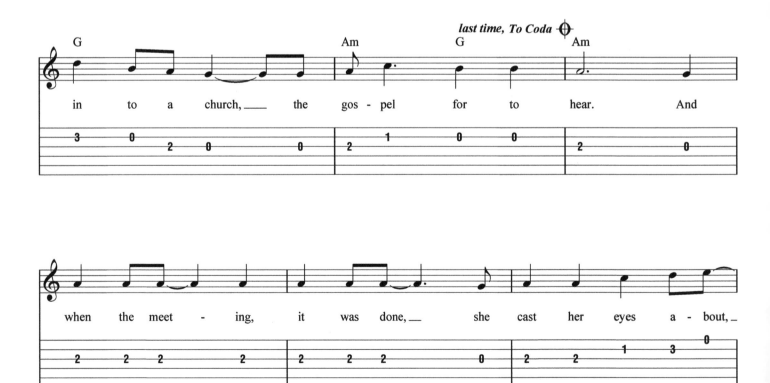

in to a church, _____ the gos - pel for to hear. And

when the meet - ing, it was done, _____ she cast her eyes a - bout, _____

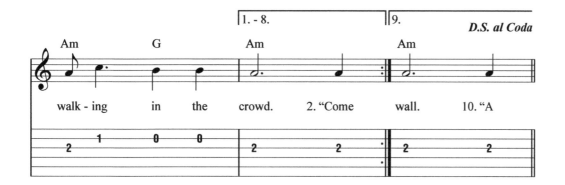

Additional Lyrics

2. "Come home with me, little Matty Groves, come home with me tonight.
   Come home with me, little Matty Groves, and sleep with me till light."
   "Oh, I can't come home, I won't come home and sleep with you tonight.
   By the rings on your fingers I can tell you are my master's wife."

3. "But if I am Lord Donald's wife, Lord Donald's not at home.
   He is out in the far cornfields bringing the yearlings home."
   And a servant who was standing by and hearing what was said,
   He swore Lord Donald, he would know before the sun would set.

4. And in his hurry to carry the news, he bent his breast and ran.
   And when he came to the broad millstream, he took off his shoes and he swam.
   Little Matty Groves, he lay down and took a little sleep.
   When he awoke, Lord Donald was standing at his feet.

5. Saying, "How do you like my feather bed, and how do you like my sheets?
   How do you like my lady, who lies in your arms asleep?"
   "Oh, well I like your feather bed, and well I like your sheets.
   But better I like your lady gay who lies in my arms asleep."

6. "Well, get up, get up," Lord Donald cried, "get up as quick as you can.
   It'll never be said in fair England that I slew a naked man."
   "Oh, I can't get up, I won't get up, I can't get up for my life.
   For you have two long beaten swords and I not a pocket knife."

7. "Well it's true I have two beaten swords and they cost me deep in the purse.
   But you will have the better of them and I will have the worse.
   And you will strike the very first blow and strike it like a man.
   I will strike the very next blow and I'll kill you if I can."

8. So Matty struck the very first blow and he hurt Lord Donald sore.
   Lord Donald struck the very next blow and Matty struck no more.
   And then Lord Donald took his wife and he sat her on his knee
   Saying, "Who do you like the best of us, Matty Groves or me?"

9. And then up spoke his own dear wife, never heard to speak so free,
   "I'd rather a kiss from dead Matty's lips than you or your finery."
   Lord Donald, he jumped up and loudly he did bawl.
   He struck his wife right through the heart and pinned her against the wall.

10. "A grave, a grave," Lord Donald cried, "to put these lovers in.
    But bury my lady at the top for she was of noble kin."

Michael Row the Boat Ashore

Traditional Folksong

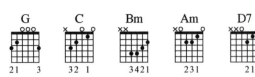

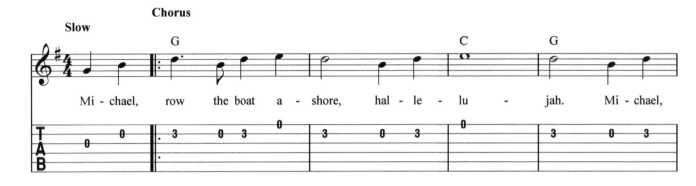

Additional Lyrics

2. Jordan River is chilly and cold, hallelujah.
   Kills the body but not the soul, hallelujah.

3. Jordan River is deep and wide, hallelujah.
   Milk and honey on the other side, hallelujah.

Nobody Knows the Trouble I've Seen

African-American Spiritual

Midnight Special

Railroad Song

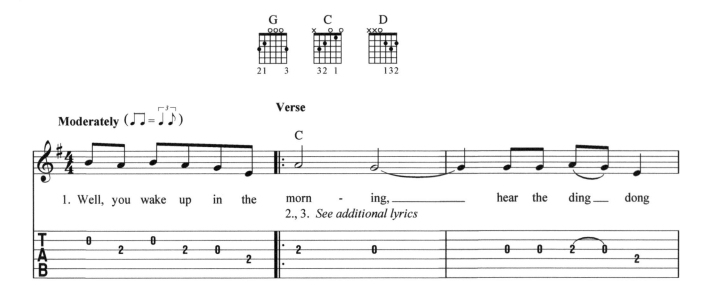

Moderately (♫ = ♪³♪)

Verse

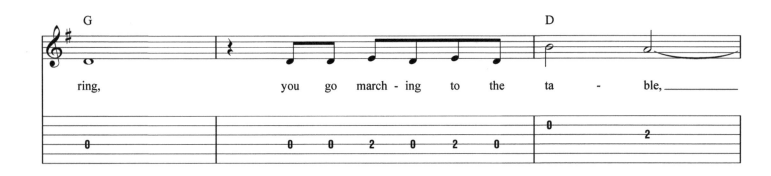

1. Well, you wake up in the morn - ing, _____ hear the ding ___ dong
2., 3. *See additional lyrics*

ring, you go march - ing to the ta - ble, _____

___ see the same ___ damn ___ thing. Well, it's on - ly one ___ ta - ble,

knife and fork ___ and a pan, and if you say a thing a-

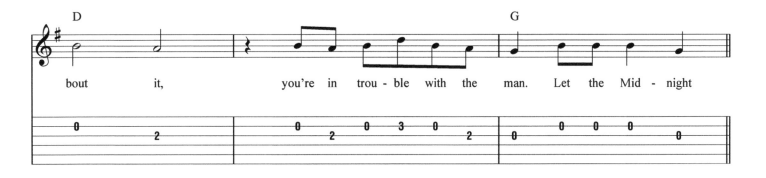

bout it, you're in trou - ble with the man. Let the Mid - night

Chorus

Spe - cial _____ shine her light ____ on me. _____

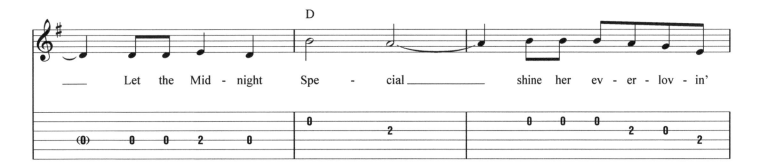

____ Let the Mid - night Spe - cial _____ shine her ev - er - lov - in'

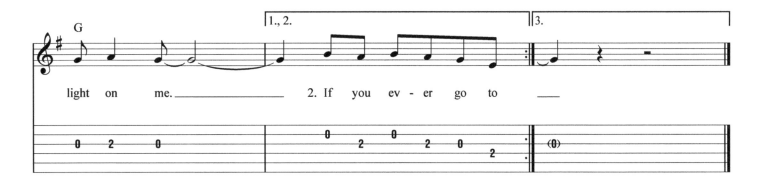

light on me. _____ 2. If you ev - er go to ____

Additional Lyrics

2. If you ever go to Houston, you'd better walk right,
   And you better not stagger, and you better not fight.
   'Cause the sheriff will arrest you, and he'll carry you down,
   And you bet your bottom dollar, you're for Sugarland bound.

3. Lord, Thelma said she loved me, but I believe she told a lie,
   'Cause she hasn't been to see me since last July.
   She brought me little coffee, she brought me little tea,
   She brought me nearly ev'rything but the jailhouse key.

My Old Kentucky Home

Words and Music by Stephen C. Foster

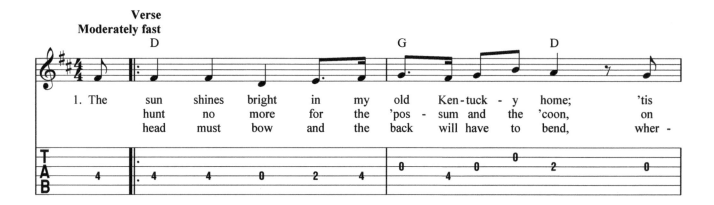

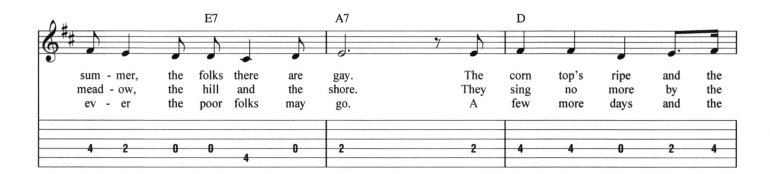

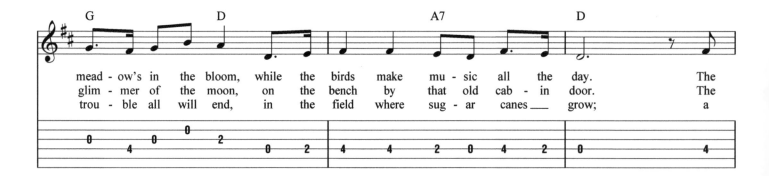

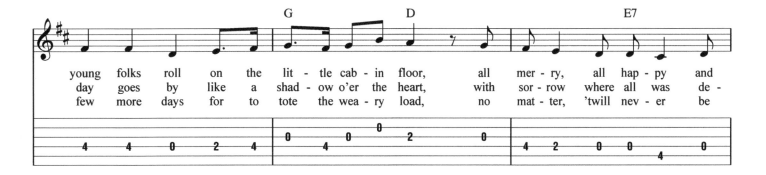

young folks roll on the lit - tle cab - in floor, all mer - ry, all hap - py and
day goes by like a shad - ow o'er the heart, with sor - row where all was de -
few more days for to tote the wea - ry load, no mat - ter, 'twill nev - er be

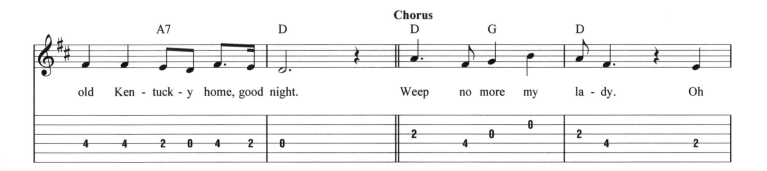

bright. By'n by hard times come a knock - ing at the door.
light. The time has come when the old friends have to part. } Then my
light. A few more days till we tot - ter on the road.

Chorus

old Ken - tuck - y home, good night. Weep no more my la - dy. Oh

weep no more to - day. We will sing one song for the old Ken - tuck - y home, for the

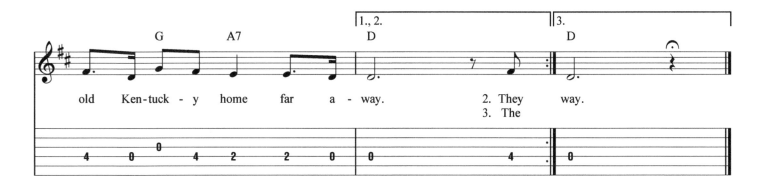

old Ken - tuck - y home far a - way. 2. They way.
3. The

Oh! Susanna

Words and Music by Stephen C. Foster

Additional Lyrics

2. It rained all night the day I left, the weather it was dry,
The sun so hot I froze to death, Susanna, don't you cry.

3. I had a dream the other night when everything was still.
I thought I saw Susanna a coming down the hill.

4. The buckwheat cake was in her mougth, the tear was in her eye.
Says I, "I'm coming from the South, Susanna, don't you cry."

The Red River Valley

Traditional American Cowboy Song

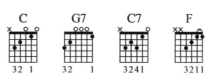

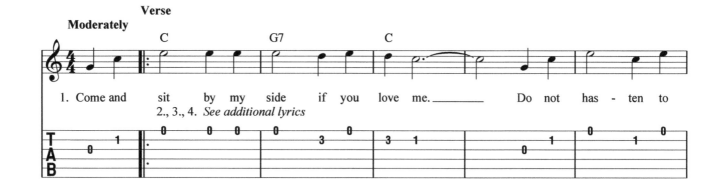

1. Come and sit by my side if you love me. _____ Do not has - ten to
2., 3., 4. *See additional lyrics*

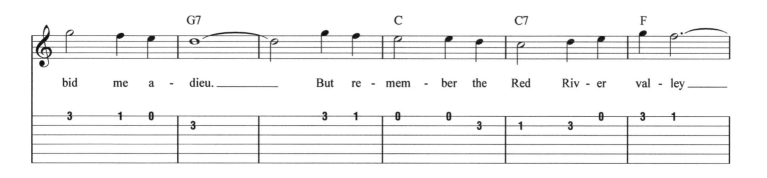

bid me a - dieu. _____ But re - mem - ber the Red Riv - er val - ley _____

_____ and the cow - boy who loves you so true. _____ 2. Won't you _____

Additional Lyrics

2. Won't you think of this valley you're leaving?
   Oh, how lonely, how sad it will be.
   Oh, think of the fond heart you're breaking,
   And the grief you are causing me.

3. From this valley they say you are going.
   When you go, may your darling go, too?
   Would you leave her behind unprotected
   When she loves no other but you?

4. I have promised you, darling, that never
   Will a word from my lips cause you pain.
   And my life, it will be yours forever,
   If you only will love me again.

Old Folks At Home
(Swanee River)

Words and Music by Stephen C. Foster

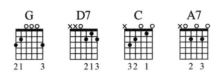

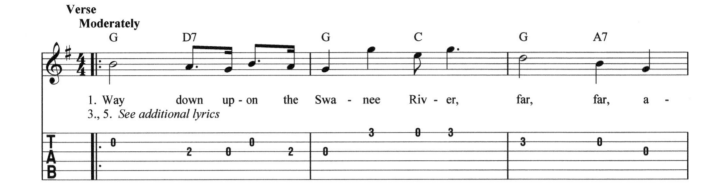

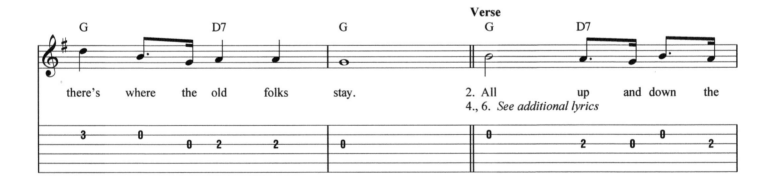

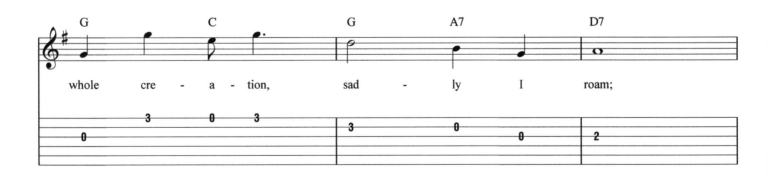

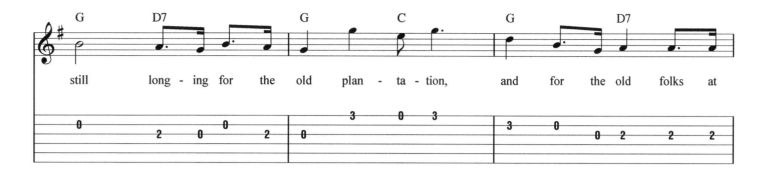

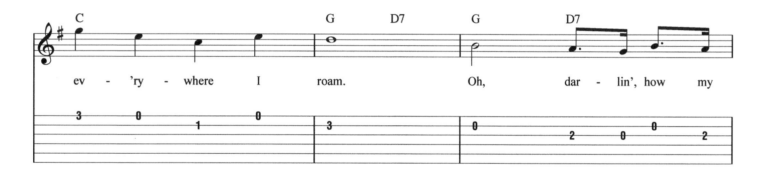

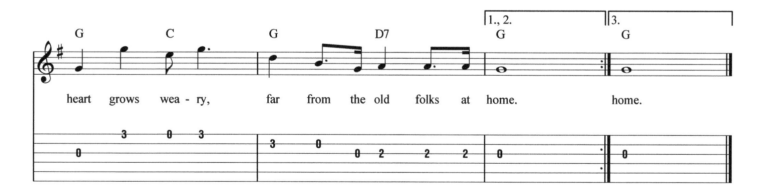

Additional Lyrics

3. All 'round the little farm I wandered
   When I was young.
   Then many happy days I squandered,
   Many the songs I sung.

4. When I was playing with my brother,
   Happy was I.
   Oh, take me to my kind old mother,
   There let me live and die.

5. One little hut among the bushes,
   One that I love.
   Still sadly to my mem'ry rushes,
   No matter where I rove.

6. When will I see the bees a humming,
   All 'roun' the comb?
   When will I hear the banjo strumming,
   Down in my good old home?

Rock Island Line

Railroad Song

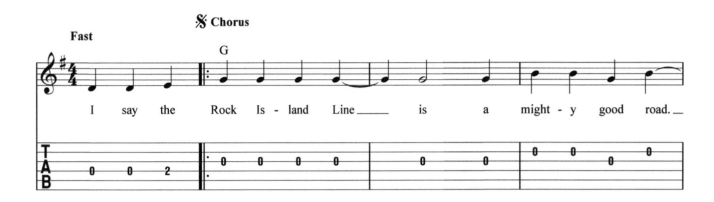

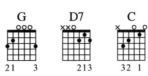

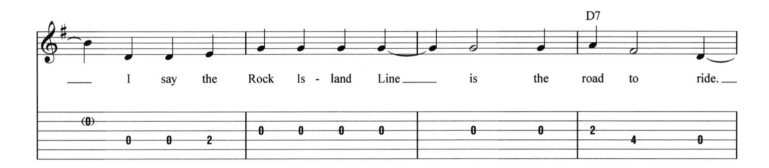

I say the Rock Is - land Line ____ is a might - y good road. ____

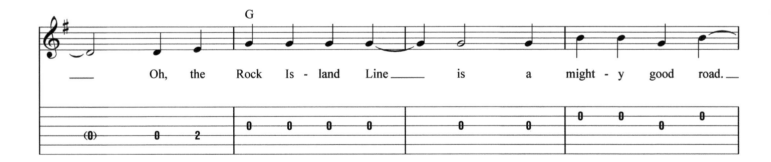

____ I say the Rock Is - land Line ____ is the road to ride. ____

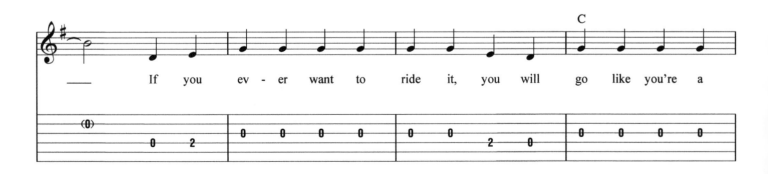

____ Oh, the Rock Is - land Line ____ is a might - y good road. ____

____ If you ev - er want to ride it, you will go like you're a

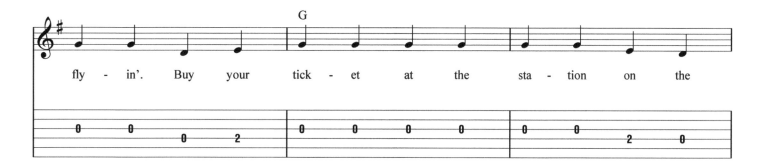

fly - in'. Buy your tick - et at the sta - tion on the

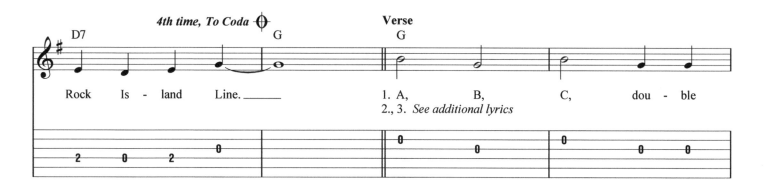

4th time, To Coda ⊕   **Verse**

Rock Is - land Line._____ 1. A, B, C, dou - ble

2., 3. *See additional lyrics*

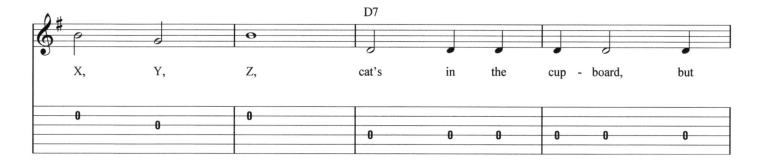

X, Y, Z, cat's in the cup - board, but

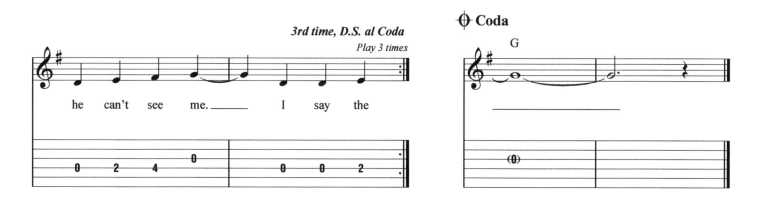

3rd time, D.S. al Coda

Play 3 times

⊕ **Coda**

he can't see me._____ I say the

_____

Additional Lyrics

2. Jesus died to save our sins,
   Glory be to God, we're going to see Him again.

3. I may be right and I may be wrong,
   I know you're gonna miss me when I am gone.

Scarborough Fair

Traditional English

Additional Lyrics

2. Tell her make me a cambric shirt,
Parsley, sage, rosemary and thyme.
Without any seam or fine needle work,
For she once was a true love of mine.

3. Tell her wash it in yonder dry well,
Parsley, sage, rosemary and thyme
Where water ne'er sprung, nor drop of rain fell,
For she once was a true love of mine.

4. Tell her to dry it on yonder thorn,
Parsley, sage, rosemary and thyme,
Which never bore blossom since Adam was born,
For she once was a true love of mine.

5. Will you find me an acre of land,
Parsley, sage, rosemary and thyme,
Between the sea foam and the sea sand?
For she once was a true love of mine.

6. Will you plough it with a lamb's horn,
Parsley, sage, rosemary and thyme,
And sow it all over with one peppercorn?
For she once was a true love of mine.

7. Will you reap it with a sickle of leather,
Parsley, sage, rosemary and thyme,
And tie it all up with a peacock's feather?
For she once was a true love of mine.

8. When you're done and finished your work,
Parsley, sage, rosemary and thyme,
Then come to me for your cambric shirt,
And you shall be a true love of mine.

She'll Be Comin' 'Round the Mountain

Traditional

Verse

Fast

1. She'll be com-in' 'round the moun-tain when she comes.
2., 3., 4. *See additional lyrics*

She'll be com-in' round the moun-tain when she comes. She'll be

com-in' round the moun-tain, she'll be com-in' 'round the moun-tain, she'll be

com-in' 'round the moun-tain when she comes. 2. She'll be

Additional Lyrics

2. She'll be drivin' six white horses when she comes.
She'll be drivin' six white horses when she comes.
She'll be drivin' six white horses,
She'll be drivin' six white horses,
She'll be drivin' six white horses when she comes.

3. Oh, we'll all go out to meet her when she comes.
Oh, we'll all go out to meet her when she comes.
Oh, we'll all go out to meet her,
Oh, we'll all go out to meet her,
Oh, we'll all go out to meet her when she comes.

4. She'll be wearin' a blue bonnet when she comes.
She'll be wearin' a blue bonnet when she comes.
She'll be wearin' a blue bonnet,
She'll be wearin' a blue bonnet,
She'll be wearin' a blue bonnet when she comes.

She Wore a Yellow Ribbon

Words and Music by George A. Norton

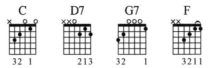

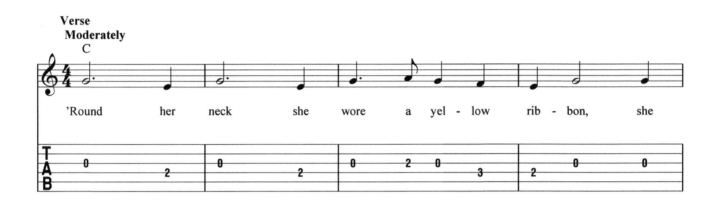

'Round her neck she wore a yel - low rib - bon, she

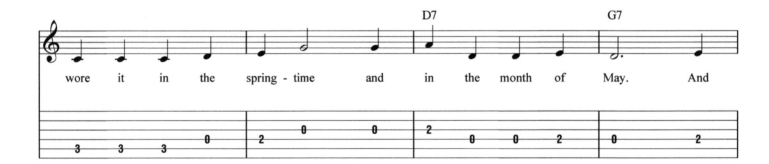

wore it in the spring - time and in the month of May. And

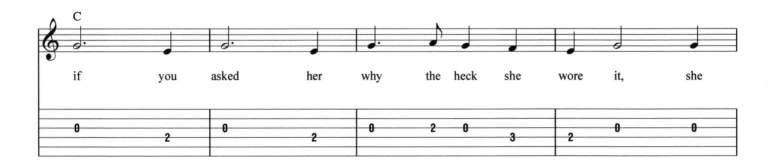

if you asked her why the heck she wore it, she

Sometimes I Feel
Like a Motherless Child

African-American Spiritual

Verse
Moderately slow

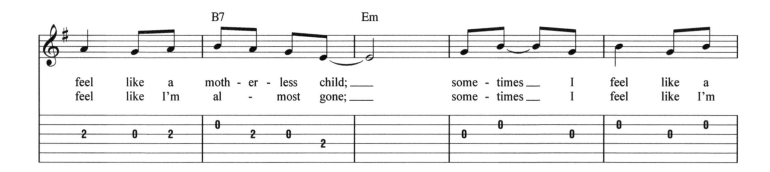

1. Some - times __ I feel like a moth - er - less child, ___ some - times __ I
2. Some - times __ I feel like I'm al - most gone, ___ some - times __ I

feel like a moth - er - less child; ___ some - times __ I feel like a
feel like I'm al - most gone; ___ some - times __ I feel like I'm

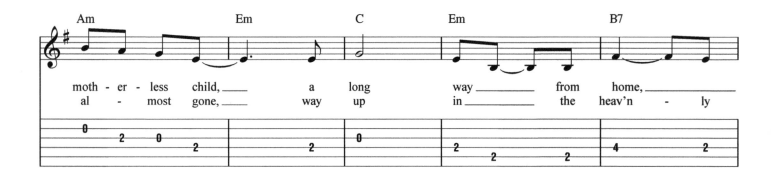

moth - er - less child, ___ a long way ___ from home, ___
al - most gone, ___ way up in ___ the heav'n - ly

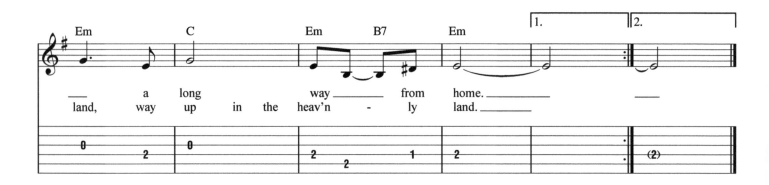

___ a long way ___ from home. ___
land, way up in the heav'n - ly land. ___

This Little Light of Mine

Traditional

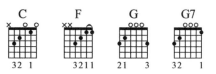

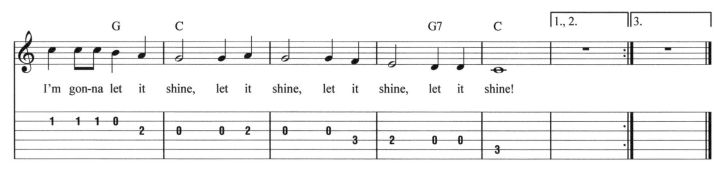

Additional Lyrics

2. Don't let Satan (blow) it out, I'm gonna let it shine. 3. Let it shine till Jesus comes, I'm gonna let it shine.
   Don't let Satan (blow) it out, I'm gonna let it shine,   Let it shine till Jesus comes, I'm gonna let it shine,
   Let it shine, let it shine, let it shine!   Let it shine, let it shine, let it shine!

There Is a Tavern in the Town

Traditional Drinking Song

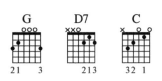

Verse
Moderately slow

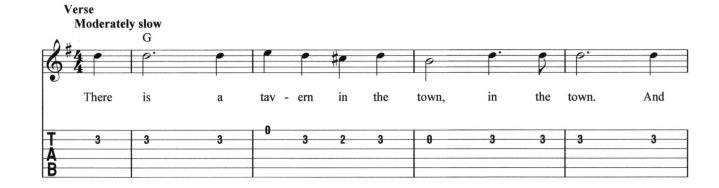

There is a tav-ern in the town, in the town. And

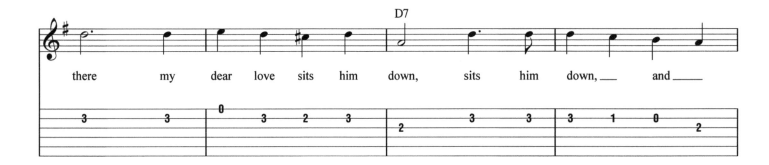

there my dear love sits him down, sits him down, ___ and ___

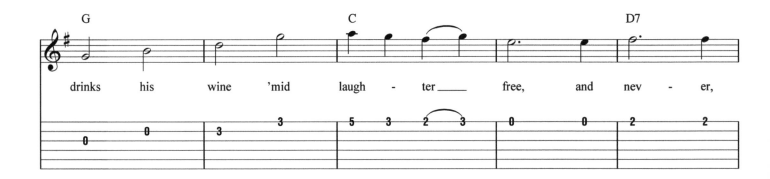

drinks his wine 'mid laugh-ter ___ free, and nev-er,

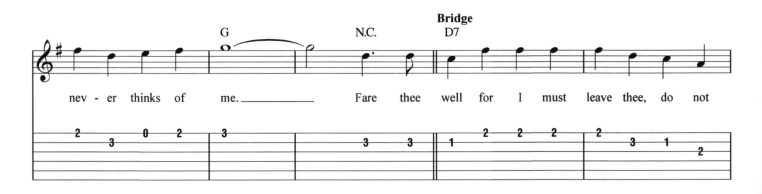

nev-er thinks of me. ___ Fare thee well for I must leave thee, do not

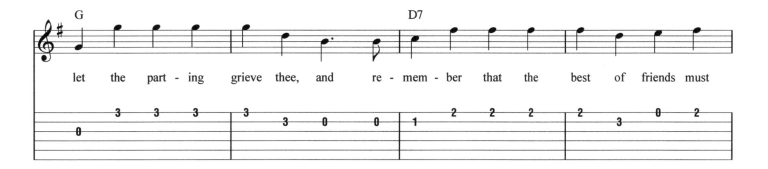

let the part - ing grieve thee, and re - mem - ber that the best of friends must

Outro-Verse

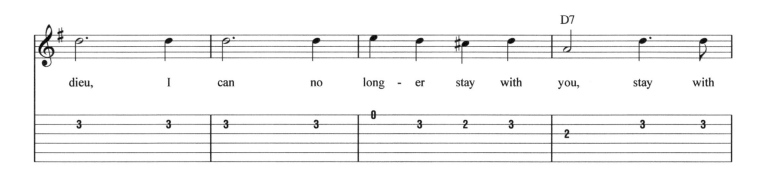

part, must part. A - dieu, a - dieu, kind friends, a - dieu, a - dieu, a -

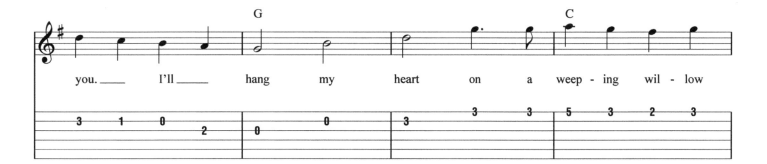

dieu, I can no long - er stay with you, stay with

you.____ I'll ____ hang my heart on a weep - ing wil - low

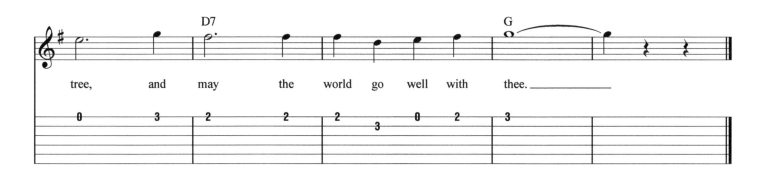

tree, and may the world go well with thee._____

This Train

Traditional

Additional Lyrics

2. This train don't carry no gamblers, this train.
   This train don't carry no gamblers, this train.
   This train don't carry no gamblers.
   No hypocrites, no midnight ramblers.
   This train is bound for glory, this train.

3. This train don't carry no liars, this train.
   This train don't carry no liars, this train.
   This train don't carry no liars.
   No hypocrites, no high flyers.
   This train is bound for glory, this train.

4. This train is built for speed now, this train.
   This train is built for speed now, this train.
   This train is built for speed now,
   Fastest train you ever did see.
   This train is bound for glory, this train.

5. This train you don't pay no transportation, this train.
   This train you don't pay no transportation, this train.
   This train you don't pay no transportation,
   No Jim Crow and no discrimination,
   This train is bound for glory, this train.

6. This train don't carry no rustlers, this train.
   This train don't carry no rustlers, this train.
   This train don't carry no rustlers,
   Sidestreet walkers, two-bit hustlers
   This train is bound for glory, this train.

The Wabash Cannon Ball

Hobo Song

Additional Lyrics

2. She came down from Birmingham one cold December day,
   As she rolled into the station, you could hear all the people say,
   There's a girl from Tennessee, she's long and she's tall.
   She came down from Birmingham on the Wabash Cannon Ball.

3. Our eastern states are dandy so the people always say,
   From New York to St. Louis and Chicago by the way.
   From the hills of Minnesota where the rippling waters fall,
   No changes can be taken on that Wabash Cannon Ball.

4. Here's to Daddy Claxton, may his name forever stand,
   And always be remembered 'round the courts of Alabam.
   His earthly race is over and the curtains 'round him fall,
   We'll carry him to vict'ry on the Wabash Cannon Ball.

5. Listen to the jingle, the rumble and the roar
   As she glides along the woodlands, through the hills and by the shore.
   Hear the mighty rush of the engine, hear the lonesome hobo squall,
   You're trav'ling through the jungles on the Wabash Cannon Ball.

Turkey in the Straw

American Folksong

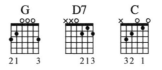

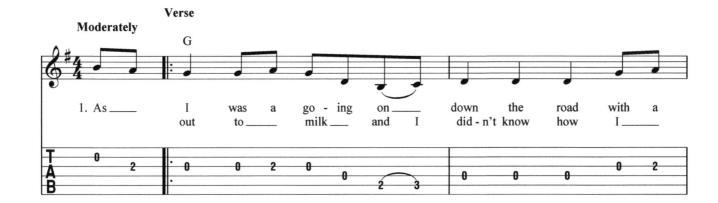

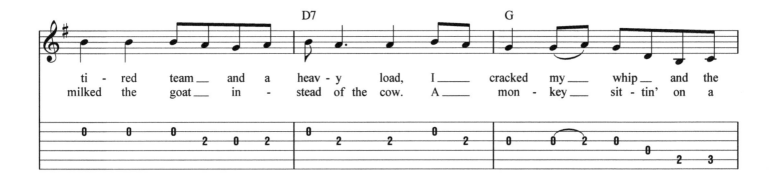

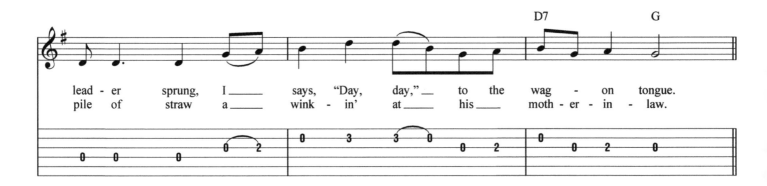

Chorus

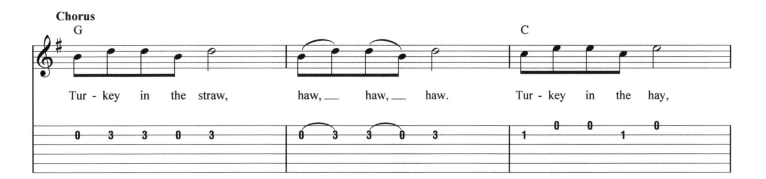

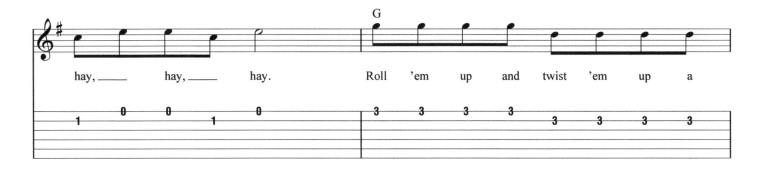

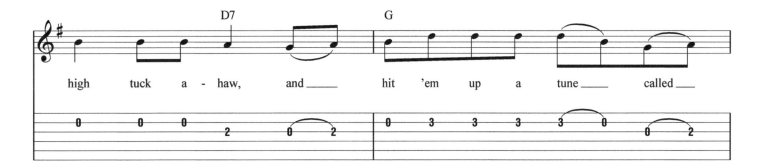

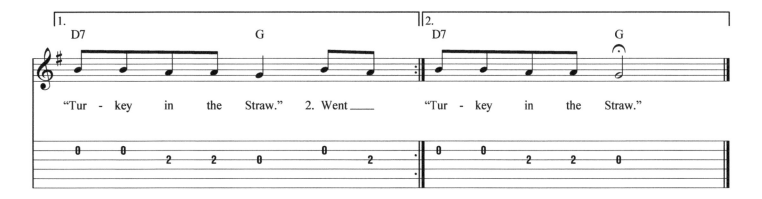

Water Is Wide

Traditional

Additional Lyrics

2. I put my hand into some soft bush,
Thinking the sweetest flower to find,
The thorn, it stuck me to the bone,
And, oh, I left that flower alone.

3. A ship there is and she sails the sea,
She's loaded deep as deep can be.
But not so deep as the love I'm in,
And I know not how to sink or swim.

4. Oh, love is handsome and love is fine,
Gay as a jewel when first it's new.
But love grows old and waxes cold
And fades away like summer dew.

5. I leaned my back against a young oak,
Thinking he was a trusty tree.
But first he bended and then he broke,
And thus did my false love to me.

When Johnny Comes Marching Home

Words and Music by Patrick Sarsfield Gilmore

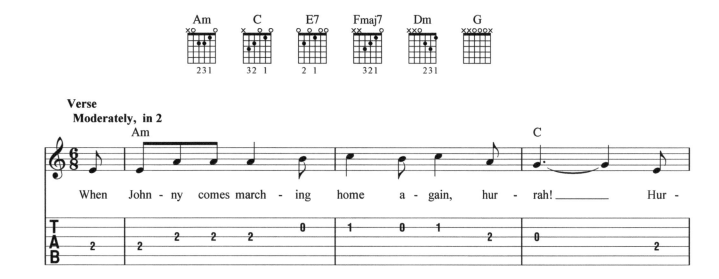

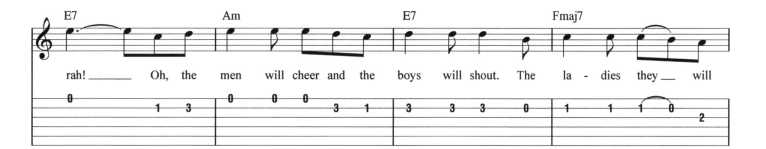

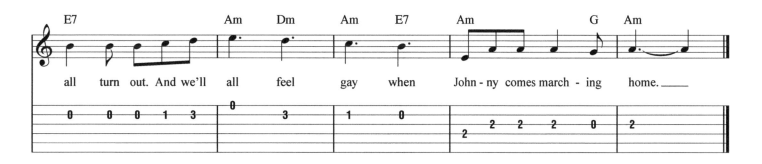

When the Saints Go Marching In

Words by Katherine E. Purvis
Music by James M. Black

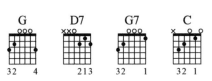

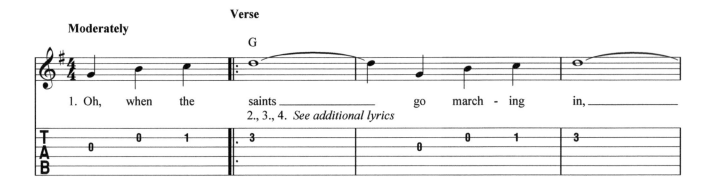

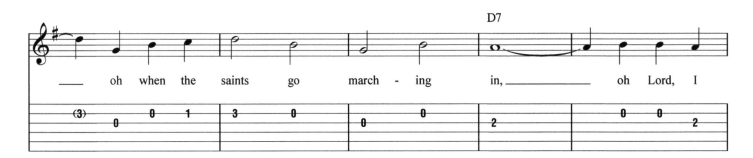

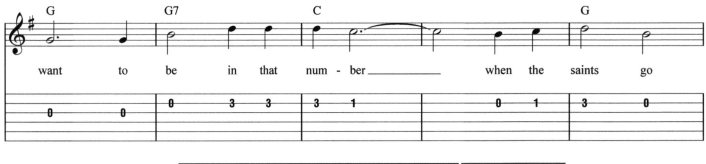

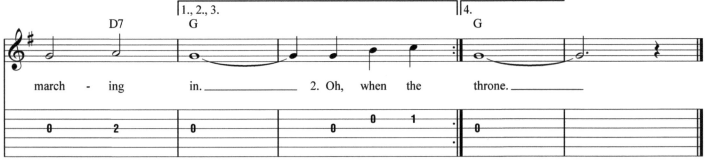

Additional Lyrics

2. Oh, when the sun refuse to shine,
Oh, when the sun refuse to shine,
Oh Lord, I want to be in that number,
When the sun refuse to shine.

3. Oh, when they crown Him Lord of all,
Oh, when they crown Him Lord of all,
Oh Lord, I want to be in that number,
When they crown Him Lord of all.

4. Oh, when they gather 'round the throne,
Oh, when they gather 'round the throne,
Oh Lord, I want to be in that number,
When they gather 'round the throne.

Wildwood Flower

Traditional

Verse

Moderately, in 2

1. Oh, I'll twine with my min - gles and wav - ing black hair,
2., 3., 4. *See additional lyrics*

with the ros - es so red and the lil - ies so fair,

and the myr - tle so bright with the em - er - ald hue, the

pale am - a - ni - ta and eyes of bright blue. 2. I will

Additional Lyrics

2. I will dance, I will sing and my life shall be gay.
   I will charm every heart, in his crown I will sway.
   When I woke from my dreaming, my idols were clay;
   Our portion of love had all flown away.

3. Oh, he taught me to love him and promised to love,
   And to cherish me over all others above.
   How my heart is now wondering, no misery can tell;
   He's left me no warning, no words of farewell.

4. Oh, he taught me to love him and called me his flower
   That was blooming to cheer him through life's dreary hour.
   Oh, I long to see him and regret the dark hour;
   He's gone and neglected this pale wildwood flower.

Will the Circle Be Unbroken

Words by Ada R. Habershon
Music by Charles H. Gabriel

Additional Lyrics

2. Lord, I told the undertaker,
   "Undertaker, please drive slow,
   For this body you are hauling,
   Lord I hate to see her go."

3. I followed close behind her,
   Tried to hold up and be brave,
   But I could not hide my sorrow
   When they laid her in the grave.

4. Went back home, Lord. My home was lonesome,
   Since my mother, she was gone.
   All my brothers, sisters, crying,
   What a home so sad and lone.

Worried Man Blues

Traditional

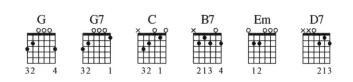

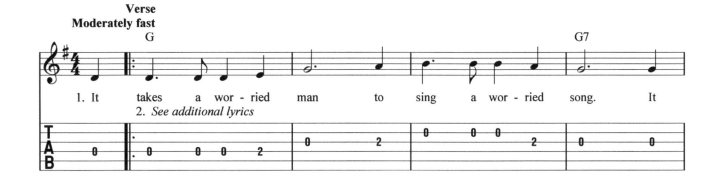

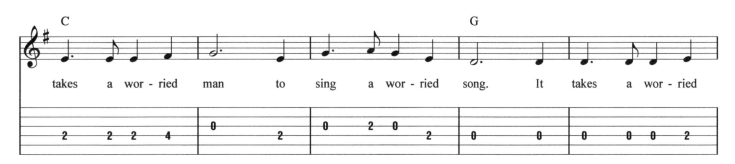

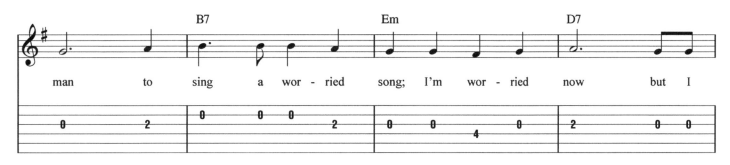

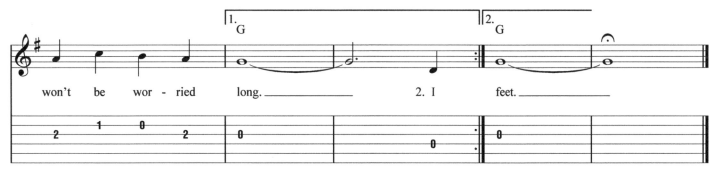

Additional Lyrics

2. I went across the river and I lay down to sleep.
I went across the river and I lay down to sleep.
I went across the river and I lay down to sleep;
When I woke up, had shackles on my feet.

The Yellow Rose of Texas

Words and Music by J.K., 1858

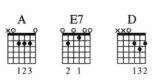

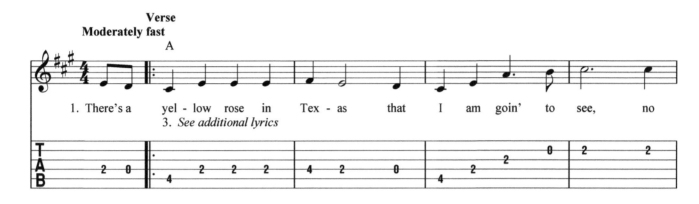

Verse
Moderately fast

1. There's a yel - low rose in Tex - as that I am goin' to see, no
3. *See additional lyrics*

oth - er fel - low loves her, no - bod - y, on - ly me. She

cried so when I left her, it like to broke my heart, and

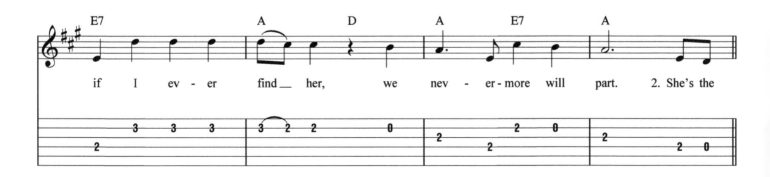

if I ev - er find __ her, we nev - er - more will part. 2. She's the

Additional Lyrics

3. Where the Rio Grande is flowing,
   And the starry skies are bright,
   She walks along the river,
   In the quiet summer night.
   She thinks, if I remember,
   When we parted long ago,
   I promised to come back again,
   And not to leave her so.

4. Oh, now I'm going to find her,
   For my heart is full of woe.
   And we'll sing the song together
   That we sang so long ago.
   We'll play the banjo gaily
   And we'll sing the songs of yore,
   And the yellow rose of Texas
   Shall be mine forevermore.

Yankee Doodle

Traditional

Additional Lyrics

2. And there we saw a thousand men
   As rich as Squire David.
   And what they wasted ev'ry day,
   I wish it could be saved.

3. And there was Captain Washington
   Upon a slapping stallion
   A giving orders to his men,
   I guess there was a million.

4. And then the feathers on his hat,
   They looked so very fine, ah!
   I wanted peskily to get
   To give to my Jemima.

5. And there I see a swamping gun
   Large as a log of maple,
   Upon a mighty little cart,
   A load for father's cattle.

6. And ev'ry time they fired it off,
   It took a horn of powder,
   It made a noise like father's gun,
   Only a nation louder.

7. An' there I see a little keg,
   Its head all made of leather;
   They knocked upon't with little sticks
   To call the folks together.

8. And Cap'n Davis had a gun,
   He kind o' clapt his hand on't
   And stuck a crooked stabbing-iron
   Upon the little end on't.

9. The troopers too, would gallop up
   And fire right in our faces.
   It scared me almost half to death
   To see them run such races.

10. It scared me so I hooked it off
    Nor stopped, as I remember,
    Nor turned about till I got home,
    Locked up in mother's chamber.

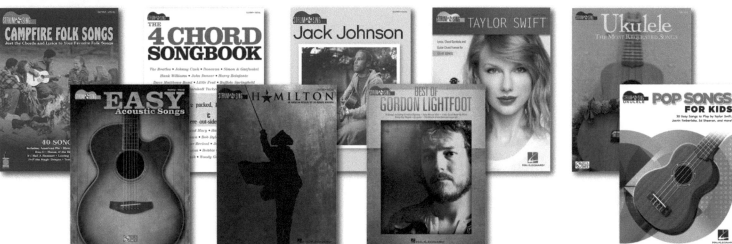

STRUM & SING

The Strum & Sing series for guitar and ukulele provides an unplugged and pared-down approach to your favorite songs – just the chords and the lyrics, with nothing fancy. These easy-to-play arrangements are designed for both aspiring and professional musicians.

GUITAR

Acoustic Classics
00191891 ....$15.99

Adele
00159855 ....$12.99

Sara Bareilles
00102354 ....$12.99

The Beatles
00172234 ....$17.99

Blues
00159335 ....$12.99

Zac Brown Band
02501620 ....$19.99

Colbie Caillat
02501725 ....$14.99

Campfire Folk Songs
02500686 ....$15.99

Chart Hits of 2014-2015
00142554 ....$12.99

Chart Hits of 2015-2016
00156248 ....$12.99

Best of Kenny Chesney
00142457 ....$14.99

Christmas Carols
00348351 ....$14.99

Christmas Songs
00171332 ....$14.99

Kelly Clarkson
00146384 ....$14.99

Coffeehouse Songs for Guitar
00285991 ....$14.99

Leonard Cohen
00265489 ....$14.99

Dear Evan Hansen
00295108 ....$16.99

John Denver Collection
02500632 ....$17.99

Disney
00233900 ....$16.99

Eagles
00157994 ....$12.99

Easy Acoustic Songs
00125478 ....$19.99

Billie Eilish
00363094 ....$14.99

The Five-Chord Songbook
02501718 ....$12.99

Folk Rock Favorites
02501669 ....$14.99

Folk Songs
02501482 ....$14.99

The Four-Chord Country Songbook
00114936 ....$15.99

The Four Chord Songbook
02501533 ....$14.99

Four Chord Songs
00249581 ....$14.99

The Greatest Showman
00278383 ....$14.99

Hamilton
00217116 ....$15.99

Hymns
02501125 ....$8.99

Jack Johnson
02500858 ....$17.99

Robert Johnson
00191890 ....$12.99

Carole King
00115243 ....$10.99

Best of Gordon Lightfoot
00139393 ....$15.99

Dave Matthews Band
02501078 ....$10.95

John Mayer
02501636 ....$19.99

The Most Requested Songs
02501748 ....$14.99

Jason Mraz
02501452 ....$14.99

**Tom Petty –
Wildflowers & All the Rest**
00362682 ....$14.99

Elvis Presley
00198890 ....$12.99

Queen
00218578 ....$12.99

Rock Around the Clock
00103625 ....$12.99

Rock Ballads
02500872 ....$9.95

Rocketman
00300469 ....$17.99

Ed Sheeran
00152016 ....$14.99

The Six-Chord Songbook
02502277 ....$12.99

Chris Stapleton
00362625 ....$19.99

Cat Stevens
00116827 ....$17.99

Taylor Swift
00159856 ....$12.99

The Three-Chord Songbook
00211634 ....$12.99

Today's Hits
00119301 ....$12.99

Top Christian Hits
00156331 ....$12.99

Top Hits of 2016
00194288 ....$12.99

Keith Urban
00118558 ....$14.99

The Who
00103667 ....$12.99

Yesterday
00301629 ....$14.99

Neil Young – Greatest Hits
00138270 ....$15.99

UKULELE

The Beatles
00233899 ....$16.99

Colbie Caillat
02501731 ....$10.99

Coffeehouse Songs
00138238 ....$14.99

John Denver
02501694 ....$14.99

Folk Rock Favorites
00114600 ....$16.99

The 4-Chord Ukulele Songbook
00114331 ....$16.99

Jack Johnson
02501702 ....$19.99

John Mayer
02501706 ....$10.99

Ingrid Michaelson
02501741 ....$12.99

The Most Requested Songs
02501453 ....$14.99

Jason Mraz
02501753 ....$14.99

Pop Songs for Kids
00284415 ....$16.99

Sing-Along Songs
02501710 ....$15.99

HAL•LEONARD®
halleonard.com
Visit our website to see full song lists
or order from your favorite retailer.

*Prices, contents and availability
subject to change without notice.*

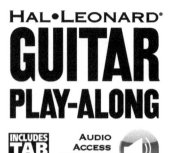

HAL·LEONARD® GUITAR PLAY-ALONG

INCLUDES TAB — AUDIO ACCESS INCLUDED

This series will help you play your favorite songs quickly and easily. Just follow the tab and listen to the audio to hear how the guitar should sound, and then play along using the separate backing tracks.

Playback tools are provided for slowing down the tempo without changing pitch and looping challenging parts. The melody and lyrics are included in the book so that you can sing or simply follow along.

1. ROCK
00699570.................$16.99

2. ACOUSTIC
00699569.................$16.99

3. HARD ROCK
00699573.................$17.99

4. POP/ROCK
00699571.................$16.99

5. THREE CHORD SONGS
00300985.................$16.99

6. '90S ROCK
00298615.................$16.99

7. BLUES
00699575.................$17.99

8. ROCK
00699585.................$16.99

9. EASY ACOUSTIC SONGS
00151708.................$16.99

10. ACOUSTIC
00699586.................$16.95

11. EARLY ROCK
0699579.................$15.99

12. ROCK POP
00291724.................$16.99

14. BLUES ROCK
00699582.................$16.99

15. R&B
00699583.................$17.99

16. JAZZ
00699584.................$16.99

17. COUNTRY
00699588.................$16.99

18. ACOUSTIC ROCK
00699577.................$15.95

20. ROCKABILLY
00699580.................$16.99

21. SANTANA
00174525.................$17.99

22. CHRISTMAS
00699600.................$15.99

23. SURF
00699635.................$16.99

24. ERIC CLAPTON
00699649.................$17.99

25. THE BEATLES
00198265.................$17.99

26. ELVIS PRESLEY
00699643.................$16.99

27. DAVID LEE ROTH
00699645.................$16.95

28. GREG KOCH
00699646.................$17.99

29. BOB SEGER
00699647.................$16.99

30. KISS
00699644.................$16.99

32. THE OFFSPRING
00699653.................$14.95

33. ACOUSTIC CLASSICS
00699656.................$17.99

34. CLASSIC ROCK
00699658.................$17.99

35. HAIR METAL
00699660.................$17.99

36. SOUTHERN ROCK
00699661.................$19.99

37. ACOUSTIC UNPLUGGED
00699662.................$22.99

38. BLUES
00699663.................$17.99

39. '80S METAL
00699664.................$17.99

40. INCUBUS
00699668.................$17.95

41. ERIC CLAPTON
00699669.................$17.99

42. COVER BAND HITS
00211597.................$16.99

43. LYNYRD SKYNYRD
00699681.................$19.99

44. JAZZ GREATS
00699689.................$16.99

45. TV THEMES
00699718.................$14.95

46. MAINSTREAM ROCK
00699722.................$16.95

47. HENDRIX SMASH HITS
00699723.................$19.99

48. AEROSMITH CLASSICS
00699724.................$17.99

49. STEVIE RAY VAUGHAN
00699725.................$17.99

50. VAN HALEN 1978-1984
00110269.................$19.99

51. ALTERNATIVE '90S
00699727.................$14.99

52. FUNK
00699728.................$15.99

53. DISCO
00699729.................$14.99

54. HEAVY METAL
00699730.................$17.99

55. POP METAL
00699731.................$14.95

57. GUNS N' ROSES
00159922.................$17.99

58. BLINK-182
00699772.................$14.95

59. CHET ATKINS
00702347.................$16.99

60. 3 DOORS DOWN
00699774.................$14.95

62. CHRISTMAS CAROLS
00699798.................$12.95

63. CREEDENCE CLEARWATER REVIVAL
00699802.................$16.99

64. OZZY OSBOURNE
00699803.................$17.99

66. THE ROLLING STONES
00699807.................$17.99

67. BLACK SABBATH
00699808.................$16.99

68. PINK FLOYD – DARK SIDE OF THE MOON
00699809.................$17.99

71. CHRISTIAN ROCK
00699824.................$14.95

72. ACOUSTIC '90S
00699827.................$14.95

73. BLUESY ROCK
00699829.................$16.99

74. SIMPLE STRUMMING SONGS
00151706.................$19.99

75. TOM PETTY
00699882.................$19.99

76. COUNTRY HITS
00699884.................$16.99

77. BLUEGRASS
00699910.................$17.99

78. NIRVANA
00700132.................$16.99

79. NEIL YOUNG
00700133.................$24.99

80. ACOUSTIC ANTHOLOGY
00700175.................$19.95

81. ROCK ANTHOLOGY
00700176.................$22.99

82. EASY ROCK SONGS
00700177.................$17.99

84. STEELY DAN
00700200.................$19.99

85. THE POLICE
00700269.................$16.99

86. BOSTON
00700465.................$16.99

87. ACOUSTIC WOMEN
00700763.................$14.99

88. GRUNGE
00700467.................$16.99

89. REGGAE
00700468.................$15.99

90. CLASSICAL POP
00700469.................$14.99

91. BLUES INSTRUMENTALS
00700505.................$17.99

92. EARLY ROCK INSTRUMENTALS
00700506.................$15.99

93. ROCK INSTRUMENTALS
00700507.................$16.99

94. SLOW BLUES
00700508.................$16.99

95. BLUES CLASSICS
00700509.................$15.99

96. BEST COUNTRY HITS
00211615.................$16.99

97. CHRISTMAS CLASSICS
00236542.................$14.99

98. ROCK BAND
00700704.................$14.95

99. ZZ TOP
00700762.................$16.99

100. B.B. KING
00700466.................$16.99

101. SONGS FOR BEGINNERS
00701917.................$14.99

102. CLASSIC PUNK
00700769.................$14.99

103. SWITCHFOOT
00700773.................$16.99

104. DUANE ALLMAN
00700846.................$17.99

105. LATIN
00700939.................$16.99

106. WEEZER
00700958.................$14.99

107. CREAM
00701069.................$16.99

108. THE WHO
00701053.................$16.99

109. STEVE MILLER
00701054.................$19.99

110. SLIDE GUITAR HITS
00701055.................$16.99

111. JOHN MELLENCAMP
00701056.................$14.99

112. QUEEN
00701052.................$16.99

113. JIM CROCE
00701058.................$17.99

114. BON JOVI
00701060.................$16.99

115. JOHNNY CASH
00701070.................$16.99

116. THE VENTURES
00701124.................$17.99

117. BRAD PAISLEY
00701224.................$16.99

118. ERIC JOHNSON
00701353.................$16.99

119. AC/DC CLASSICS
00701356.................$17.99

120. PROGRESSIVE ROCK
00701457.................$14.99

121. U2
00701508.................$16.99

122. CROSBY, STILLS & NASH
00701610.................$16.99

123. LENNON & McCARTNEY ACOUSTIC
00701614.................$16.99

124. SMOOTH JAZZ
00200664.................$16.99

125. JEFF BECK
00701687.................$17.99

126. BOB MARLEY
00701701.................$17.99

127. 1970S ROCK
00701739.................$16.99

128. 1960S ROCK
00701740.................$14.99

129. MEGADETH
00701741.................$17.99

130. IRON MAIDEN
00701742.................$17.99

131. 1990S ROCK
00701743.................$14.99

132. COUNTRY ROCK
00701757.................$15.99

133. TAYLOR SWIFT
00701894.................$16.99

134. AVENGED SEVENFOLD
00701906.................$16.99

135. MINOR BLUES
00151350.................$17.99

136. GUITAR THEMES
00701922.................$14.99

137. IRISH TUNES
00701966.................$15.99

138. BLUEGRASS CLASSICS
00701967.................$17.99

139. GARY MOORE
00702370.................$16.99

140. MORE STEVIE RAY VAUGHAN
00702396.................$17.99

141. ACOUSTIC HITS
00702401.................$16.99

142. GEORGE HARRISON
00237697.................$17.99

143. SLASH
00702425.................$19.99

144. DJANGO REINHARDT
00702531.................$16.99

145. DEF LEPPARD
00702532.................$19.99

146. ROBERT JOHNSON
00702533.................$16.99

147. SIMON & GARFUNKEL
14041591.................$16.99

148. BOB DYLAN
14041592.................$16.99

149. AC/DC HITS
14041593.................$17.99

150. ZAKK WYLDE
02501717.................$19.99

151. J.S. BACH
02501730.................$16.99

152. JOE BONAMASSA
02501751.................$19.99

153. RED HOT CHILI PEPPERS
00702990.................$19.99

155. ERIC CLAPTON – FROM THE ALBUM UNPLUGGED
00703085.................$16.99

156. SLAYER
00703770.................$19.99

157. FLEETWOOD MAC
00101382.................$17.99

159. WES MONTGOMERY
00102593.................$19.99

160. T-BONE WALKER
00102641.................$17.99

161. THE EAGLES – ACOUSTIC
00102659.................$17.99

162. THE EAGLES HITS
00102667.................$17.99

163. PANTERA
00103036.................$17.99

164. VAN HALEN 1986-1995
00110270.................$17.99

165. GREEN DAY
00210343.................$17.99

166. MODERN BLUES
00700764.................$16.99

167. DREAM THEATER
00111938.................$24.99

168. KISS
00113421.................$17.99

169. TAYLOR SWIFT
00115982.................$16.99

170. THREE DAYS GRACE
00117337.................$16.99

171. JAMES BROWN
00117420.................$16.99

172. THE DOOBIE BROTHERS
00116970.................$16.99

173. TRANS-SIBERIAN ORCHESTRA
00119907.................$19.99

174. SCORPIONS
00122119.................$16.99

175. MICHAEL SCHENKER
00122127.................$17.99

176. BLUES BREAKERS WITH JOHN MAYALL & ERIC CLAPTON
00122132.................$19.99

177. ALBERT KING
00123271.................$16.99

178. JASON MRAZ
00124165.................$17.99

179. RAMONES
00127073.................$16.99

180. BRUNO MARS
00129706.................$16.99

181. JACK JOHNSON
00129854.................$16.99

182. SOUNDGARDEN
00138161.................$17.99

183. BUDDY GUY
00138240.................$17.99

184. KENNY WAYNE SHEPHERD
00138258.................$17.99

185. JOE SATRIANI
00139457.................$17.99

186. GRATEFUL DEAD
00139459.................$17.99

187. JOHN DENVER
00140839.................$17.99

188. MÖTLEY CRUE
00141145.................$17.99

189. JOHN MAYER
00144350.................$17.99

190. DEEP PURPLE
00146152.................$17.99

191. PINK FLOYD CLASSICS
00146164.................$17.99

192. JUDAS PRIEST
00151352.................$17.99

193. STEVE VAI
00156028.................$19.99

194. PEARL JAM
00157925.................$17.99

195. METALLICA: 1983-1988
00234291.................$19.99

196. METALLICA: 1991-2016
00234292.................$19.99

HAL•LEONARD®

For complete songlists, visit
Hal Leonard online at
www.halleonard.com

Prices, contents, and availability subject to
change without notice.

1120
9/12; 397

EASY GUITAR WITH NOTES & TAB

This series features simplified arrangements with notes, tab, chord charts, and strum and pick patterns.

MIXED FOLIOS

00702287	Acoustic	$16.99
00702002	Acoustic Rock Hits for Easy Guitar	$15.99
00702166	All-Time Best Guitar Collection	$19.99
00702232	Best Acoustic Songs for Easy Guitar	$14.99
00119835	Best Children's Songs	$16.99
00702233	Best Hard Rock Songs	$15.99
00703055	The Big Book of Nursery Rhymes & Children's Songs	$16.99
00698978	Big Christmas Collection	$17.99
00702394	Bluegrass Songs for Easy Guitar	$12.99
00289632	Bohemian Rhapsody	$17.99
00703387	Celtic Classics	$14.99
00224808	Chart Hits of 2016-2017	$14.99
00267383	Chart Hits of 2017-2018	$14.99
00334293	Chart Hits of 2019-2020	$16.99
00702149	Children's Christian Songbook	$9.99
00702028	Christmas Classics	$8.99
00101779	Christmas Guitar	$14.99
00702185	Christmas Hits	$10.99
00702141	Classic Rock	$8.95
00159642	Classical Melodies	$12.99
00253933	Disney/Pixar's Coco	$16.99
00702203	CMT's 100 Greatest Country Songs	$29.99
00702283	The Contemporary Christian Collection	$16.99
00196954	Contemporary Disney	$19.99
00702239	Country Classics for Easy Guitar	$22.99
00702257	Easy Acoustic Guitar Songs	$14.99
00702280	Easy Guitar Tab White Pages	$29.99
00702041	Favorite Hymns for Easy Guitar	$10.99
00222701	Folk Pop Songs	$14.99
00126894	Frozen	$14.99
00333922	Frozen 2	$14.99
00702286	Glee	$16.99
00702160	The Great American Country Songbook	$16.99
00267383	Great American Gospel for Guitar	$12.99
00702050	Great Classical Themes for Easy Guitar	$8.99
00702116	Greatest Hymns for Guitar	$10.99
00275088	The Greatest Showman	$17.99
00148030	Halloween Guitar Songs	$14.99
00702273	Irish Songs	$12.99
00192503	Jazz Classics for Easy Guitar	$14.99
00702275	Jazz Favorites for Easy Guitar	$15.99
00702274	Jazz Standards for Easy Guitar	$17.99
00702162	Jumbo Easy Guitar Songbook	$19.99
00232285	La La Land	$16.99
00702258	Legends of Rock	$14.99
00702189	MTV's 100 Greatest Pop Songs	$24.95
00702272	1950s Rock	$15.99
00702271	1960s Rock	$15.99
00702270	1970s Rock	$16.99
00702269	1980s Rock	$15.99
00702268	1990s Rock	$19.99
00109725	Once	$14.99
00702187	Selections from O Brother Where Art Thou?	$19.99
00702178	100 Songs for Kids	$14.99
00702515	Pirates of the Caribbean	$16.99
00702125	Praise and Worship for Guitar	$10.99
00287930	Songs from *A Star Is Born, The Greatest Showman, La La Land*, and More Movie Musicals	$16.99
00702285	Southern Rock Hits	$12.99
00156420	Star Wars Music	$14.99
00121535	30 Easy Celtic Guitar Solos	$15.99
00702156	3-Chord Rock	$12.99
00702220	Today's Country Hits	$12.99
00244654	Top Hits of 2017	$14.99
00283786	Top Hits of 2018	$14.99
00702294	Top Worship Hits	$15.99
00702255	VH1's 100 Greatest Hard Rock Songs	$29.99
00702175	VH1's 100 Greatest Songs of Rock and Roll	$27.99
00702253	Wicked	$12.99

ARTIST COLLECTIONS

00702267	AC/DC for Easy Guitar	$15.99
00702598	Adele for Easy Guitar	$15.99
00156221	Adele – 25	$16.99
00702040	Best of the Allman Brothers	$16.99
00702865	J.S. Bach for Easy Guitar	$14.99
00702169	Best of The Beach Boys	$12.99
00702292	The Beatles — 1	$19.99
00125796	Best of Chuck Berry	$15.99
00702201	The Essential Black Sabbath	$12.95
00702250	blink-182 — Greatest Hits	$16.99
02501615	Zac Brown Band — The Foundation	$19.99
02501621	Zac Brown Band — You Get What You Give	$16.99
00702043	Best of Johnny Cash	$16.99
00702090	Eric Clapton's Best	$12.99
00702086	Eric Clapton — from the Album Unplugged	$15.99
00702202	The Essential Eric Clapton	$15.99
00702053	Best of Patsy Cline	$15.99
00222697	Very Best of Coldplay – 2nd Edition	$14.99
00702229	The Very Best of Creedence Clearwater Revival	$15.99
00702145	Best of Jim Croce	$15.99
00702219	David Crowder*Band Collection	$12.95
00702278	Crosby, Stills & Nash	$12.99
14042809	Bob Dylan	$14.99
00702276	Fleetwood Mac — Easy Guitar Collection	$16.99
00139462	The Very Best of Grateful Dead	$15.99
00702136	Best of Merle Haggard	$14.99
00702227	Jimi Hendrix — Smash Hits	$19.99
00702288	Best of Hillsong United	$12.99
00702236	Best of Antonio Carlos Jobim	$15.99
00702245	Elton John — Greatest Hits 1970–2002	$17.99
00129855	Jack Johnson	$16.99
00702204	Robert Johnson	$12.99
00702234	Selections from Toby Keith — 35 Biggest Hits	$12.95
00702003	Kiss	$16.99
00110578	Best of Kutless	$12.99
00702216	Lynyrd Skynyrd	$16.99
00702182	The Essential Bob Marley	$14.99
00146081	Maroon 5	$14.99
00121925	Bruno Mars – Unorthodox Jukebox	$12.99
00702248	Paul McCartney — All the Best	$14.99
00702129	Songs of Sarah McLachlan	$12.95
00125484	The Best of MercyMe	$12.99
02501316	Metallica — Death Magnetic	$19.99
00702209	Steve Miller Band — Young Hearts (Greatest Hits)	$12.95
00124167	Jason Mraz	$15.99
00702096	Best of Nirvana	$15.99
00702211	The Offspring — Greatest Hits	$12.95
00138026	One Direction	$14.99
00702030	Best of Roy Orbison	$16.99
00702144	Best of Ozzy Osbourne	$14.99
00702279	Tom Petty	$12.99
00102911	Pink Floyd	$16.99
00702139	Elvis Country Favorites	$17.99
00702293	The Very Best of Prince	$16.99
00699415	Best of Queen for Guitar	$15.99
00109279	Best of R.E.M.	$14.99
00702208	Red Hot Chili Peppers — Greatest Hits	$16.99
00198960	The Rolling Stones	$16.99
00174793	The Very Best of Santana	$14.99
00702196	Best of Bob Seger	$15.99
00146046	Ed Sheeran	$17.99
00702252	Frank Sinatra — Nothing But the Best	$17.99
00702010	Best of Rod Stewart	$16.99
00702049	Best of George Strait	$14.99
00702259	Taylor Swift for Easy Guitar	$15.99
00254499	Taylor Swift – Easy Guitar Anthology	$19.99
00702260	Taylor Swift — Fearless	$14.99
00139727	Taylor Swift — 1989	$17.99
00115960	Taylor Swift — Red	$16.99
00253667	Taylor Swift — Reputation	$17.99
00702290	Taylor Swift — Speak Now	$16.99
00702223	Chris Tomlin—Arriving	$16.99
00232849	Chris Tomlin Collection – 2nd Edition	$12.95
00702226	Chris Tomlin — See the Morning	$12.95
00148643	Train	$14.99
00702427	U2 — 18 Singles	$16.99
00702108	Best of Stevie Ray Vaughan	$16.99
00279005	The Who	$14.99
00702123	Best of Hank Williams	$15.99
00194548	Best of John Williams	$14.99
00702111	Stevie Wonder — Guitar Collection	$9.95
00702228	Neil Young — Greatest Hits	$15.99
00119133	Neil Young — Harvest	$14.99

Prices, contents and availability subject to change without notice.

Visit Hal Leonard online at **halleonard.com**